A Guide For Selecting Computers and Software

A Guide For Selecting Computers and Software For Small Businesses

By
Paul G. Enockson

Reston Publishing Co., Inc.
A Prentice-Hall Company
Reston, Virginia

Library of Congress Cataloging in Publication Data

Enockson, Paul G.
   A guide for selecting computers and software for
small businesses.

   Bibliography: p.
   1. Small business—Data processing.   2. Computers—
Purchasing.   3. Electronic digital computers—Purchasing.
I. Title.
HF 5548.2.E56   1983   001.64′04′0687   82-21478
ISBN 0-8359-2641-9
ISBN 0-9359-2642-7 (case)

© 1983 by Reston Publishing Company
A Prentice-Hall Company
Reston, Virginia 22090

10   9   8   7   6   5   4   3   2   1

Printed in the United States of America

This publication is designed to provide the author's opinion
regarding the subject matter covered. It is sold with the
understanding that the publisher or author is not engaged
in rendering legal or accounting services. If legal advice or
other expert assistance is required, the services of a competent professional person should be sought.

Paul G. Enockson
Pinnacle Software Systems
P.O. Box 1220
Ft. Collins, Colorado
303-224-5061

Interior design by Dan McCauley

*To the small businesses of America, the
heart of our free enterprise system.*

Contents

the Sales Pitch?, *45;* What Has Been the Response to Any Problems Encountered?, *45;* Are They Knowledgeable in General Business Practices?, *45*; Did They Help You With the Conversion?, *46*; Did They Work Well With Your Employees?, *46*; Were There Any Hidden Costs?, *46* Have They Completed the Job to Your Satisfaction?, *46*; If You Had It to Do All Over Again, Would You?, *46*; Would It Be Possible to Stop By and See Your System?, *47.*

Have You Obtained at Least Three References?, *50;* Does the Manufacturer Provide On-Site Maintenance?, *50*; Where is the Location of the Hardware Maintenance?, *50;* Computer Maintenance Cost, Duration, and Availability?, *51*; Is There a Replacement Machine Available?, *51*; Will the Computer Handle Your Volumes?, *51*; Is There Enough Storage Capacity for Your Data?, *51*; Is the Storage Capacity Expandable?, *51*; Will There Be Hardware Training at Your Office?, *52*; Are There Training Seminars?, *52*; Have You Reviewed the Training Manuals?, *52*; Does the Manufacturer Provide Software?, *52*; Does the Computer Require Any Special Wiring?, *52*; Does the Manufacturer Provide Utilities?, *52* Is the Computer Upward Compatible?, *53*; Is There a Toll-Free Number to Call for Computer Problems?, *53*; Is There an Error Book and Can I Understand It?, *53.*

How Long Has Your Computer Been in Operation?, *56*; What Applications Does Your Computer Have?, *56*; Do You Plan to Add Other Applications?, *56*; How Much of the Day Is the Computer Being Used?, *56*; Has the Computer Proved Reliable?, *57*; Has the Computer Ever Been Completely Down?, *57*; How Long Did It Take the Maintenance Man to Respond?, *57*; How Far Away Is Your Maintenance Man?, *57*; Is There Another Machine Close By?, *57*; Has the Repair Service Been Adequate?, *58*; Who Operates the Computer?, *58*; Is the Computer Easy to Learn to Use?, *58*; Who Supplied the Software?, *58*; Was the Installation Harder Than Expected?, *58*; Can You Stop

Preface

My career in the data processing field started in February of 1961, back when it took entire buildings to house computers which accomplished what the small desk-top computers can do today. I spent almost ten years with a large programming firm that dealt primarily with government contracts for sophisticated data processing systems.

In 1971, I started my own business providing data processing services to small businesses. At that time, computers were still too expensive for individual small businesses to own. Hence, "Service Bureaus" came about, which were simply companies which provided computer services for a wide variety of clients. The service bureaus provided the computer and the computer programs necessary to process these clients' data.

Not until the spring of 1978 did the cost of small business computers become affordable to a wide variety of businesses. At that time I focused my attention on this new approach to solving the needs of the small business through the use of "in-house" computers. Since then, I have installed, or assisted in the installation of, over 200 applications (including Accounts Receivable, General Ledger, Accounts Payable, Payroll, Inventory Control, Billing, and Sales Analysis), providing a wide range of solutions to problems facing the small business. I designed the systems, wrote the programs and supporting user documentation, trained user personnel, and ongoing support to installed clients.

My experience with these clients prompted my basic idea for writing *A Guide for Selecting Computers and Software for Small Businesses*. Seeing their mistakes pointed out to me the need for a practical, step-by-step procedure that could be used by the small business community in the transition to computerization.

Small businesses of today are caught between the proverbial "rock and a hard place." On one hand, they are trying desperately to make an honest living at something they enjoy, and finding it more difficult with each passing year. Rapid changes in our economic system, coupled with increased taxation and regulation, strain the capacities of these businesses to effectively compete in the marketplace. Changes in inventory costs, wages, overhead, etc., make it imperative that these businesses have available to them the information they need to make decisions rapidly concerning pricing, inventory quantities, wages and a wide range of other critical information.

On the other hand they are, for the most part, very skeptical about "automating" their businesses. Horror stories abound concerning businesses which have lost thousands of dollars or, worse yet, have gone bankrupt in their attempts to automate. And it does happen.

With the decline in the cost of small business computers, a vast (and virtually untapped) market has developed. The industry is moving so fast that it is difficult for the trained data processing professional to keep up with it. Given this fact, how then can small businesses be expected to be able to make intelligent decisions in this ever-changing field? The truth is, they can't. They must rely on the good intentions of the individuals and companies selling the computers and the programs that run them. If they are fortunate, everything turns out fine; if not, they become part of the ever-increasing group for whom the horror stories become a reality.

A computer is not a "cure all" for whatever ails a business. It cannot cure poor management practices, improper product selection and packaging, or an inferior sales approach. Rather, a computer can provide the information needed by the business to make the decisions that can provide the medicine necessary to effect a cure.

In my association with small businesses, I found that a large number of them did not really know what they wanted, needed, or what was available. Without "clear" definitions at the beginning of any project involving computers, the results can be less than expected. Misunderstandings on both sides usually develop, and in the end both parties lose. Those who take the step, roll up their sleeves, and approach the project of automation with the firm belief that it CAN and will be done are the ones who share in the rewards that automation can, and does, bring.

I have first hand experience working with these businesses and seeing their excitement and pleasure at the results that were achieved by automating vital business activities. In one case, a businessman told me, excitedly, that he had paid for both computer and programs by simply having the "automatic" capability to charge overdue accounts interest. And, they *paid* the interest.

The best part of his story was that he had accomplished all of this after only three months' use of his new system!

In another case, the ability to isolate slow-moving inventory items allowed a business the information they needed to negotiate with the supplier for return of the merchandise. The credit they received allowed them to take advantage of a special being offered by the supplier, thus saving thousands of dollars.

I could cite many more examples of businesses saving thousands of dollars and hundreds of hours of time by automating. The point is that you, too, can achieve success in automating your own business by following the procedures outlined in this book. Though it will require an initial investment of your time, the results will more than compensate for your efforts. You can look forward to an end to those long evenings and weekends at the office. Instead, you'll be able to spend more time with your family or pursue whatever hobbies or interest you enjoy. You will have the *time*.

The methods and procedures used in *A Guide for Selecting Computers and Software for Small Businesses*, as well as the sequence, are of my own development and are addressed to the businessman with little or no training in the field of data processing. The approach used to present the information is of my own design, and the final conclusions and any errors or omissions are solely mine. Ultimate decisions and responsibility rest with you. However, if you follow the procedures and suggestions contained in this book, apply them, and make the critical commitments of time and money, you will surely be successful.

Paul G. Enockson

Introduction

In 1978, Radio Shack reportedly sold 10,500 personal computers. Their sales campaign was aimed directly at you, the consumer. All this activity was not lost on the other computer companies. In the spring of 1979, IBM began marketing its 5110, modified to meet small business needs. A little more than a year later, in the spring of 1980, they introduced the 5120 and now, in July of 1981, the System/23. The race is on!

But, it's not all a bed of roses. There have always been salesmen who promised what sounded like the "ideal" solution and buyers who were surprised when the equipment delivered a lot less than expected. And, the number of first-time users who are unhappy with their "ideal" solution is increasing rapidly.

The major problem is the ever-expanding number of first-time users. These are the small companies who have a need but not the in-house expertise to evaluate these computers and software packages.

The declining prices of the computers have left little margin of profit for the hardware manufacturers to pay for the necessary assistance these first-time users so desperately need.

This has left a void which is being filled with third parties, independent programmers, and small software vendors who sell their programs and assistance to these first-time users. Even with this assistance, the end user is likely to end up with something less than expected. It is estimated that 50 percent of all first-time users are dissatisfied, or angry with the end results. It's a problem, and one that is not going to go away.

This book should give you two things: first, a clear understanding of how to determine your own requirements and what you really want from a computer system and, second, an approach to be used in securing the best hardware and software match that fits your own requirements. While delivering these two critical benefits, the book also explains the questions you must ask yourself, the hardware salesman, and the software vendor. It is written in terms you can understand, and provides a crash course in the methods and procedures you should use in selecting your entire computer system.

However, this book is *not* an endorsement of any particular computer or software system. Both of these industries are changing so rapidly that it would take a staff of one hundred people working full time to keep up with it. Rather, this book is a methodology for assisting you in determining your needs, the steps necessary for the selection of a computer to fit those needs, and, finally, selection of the computer programs that will come the closest to meeting your needs.

I have tried to keep the technical terms to a minimum. However, you may as well become accustomed to some of them. With this in mind, I have included a glossary of these terms, and their first reference within the text is italicized.

A word of caution. You should follow the procedures as outlined in this book as closely as possible. If there are questions and/or procedures that do not apply to your particular situation, simply skip over them. The immediate and long-range benefits you will gain by pursuing the principles outlined in this book will result in the accomplishment of installing a computer system in your business that will satisfy your business needs, and one of which you will be proud.

A Guide For Selecting Computers and Software

CHAPTER 1

Start

Let's Begin!

Given specific instructions, a _computer_ can perform an unlimited variety of jobs; it can solve a complex mathematical problem, calculate and post interest to a bill and print it, monitor sophisticated electronic equipment, predict football game outcomes, guide space ships, and provide rapid responses to questions. However, no computer can think for itself. It can only do those functions "told" to it by an individual in a prescribed order. The individuals who provide these instructions to the computers are called _programmers_, and the instructions they give to the computer are referred to as _programming_. This programming is just as important, if not more so, than the operating capabilities of the computer _hardware_ itself.

Programming a computer can be quite complex. Since a computer must go through many steps in order to solve a specific problem, some problems can be solved as quickly without a computer (such as a simple multiplication of 10 times 10).

Although programming a computer to make this calculation would not be difficult, what about the writing of instructions required to determine when your inventory items fall below minimums, to calculate order requirements, to print a purchase order, and to update the inventory file based on the quantities that were ordered? Or the instructions required to capitalize any state name that appeared in the text of a newspaper or magazine?

In order to program a computer to solve any of these problems, you would first have to know more about the problem itself, analyze it and break it down into several parts or steps. As a simple example to illustrate how many parts there can be to a problem, consider an ordinary activity like putting on your pants. How many insignificant motions are involved in acomplishing this task? Get pants. Put right foot in right trouser leg. Pull on right leg. Put left foot in left trouser leg. Pull on left leg. Pull pants to waist. Snap top snap. Zip up front.

If we count the major actions involved in the simple act of putting on a pair of pants, we find that it takes *eight* major steps. But, remember, every one of these major actions involves several subactions: bend over, bend leg, push leg, bend arm, move hand, stand up, close fingers, and so on.

As human beings, we can perform this action with our own computer—our brain—by simply giving it the signal "put on pants." The logical sequence of actions required to complete this task has been programmed (learned) and stored in our memory to be used repeatedly, whenever the proper command is given. The same procedure and results apply to a computer.

Flow Diagrams

The approach used in this book is the same as solving a computer problem. First came the major definition of the problem—how can a small business with little or no background in a relatively new field make the right decision about automation? This definition resulted in the identification of two major problems: 1.) Selecting a set of programs commonly referred to as a system and 2.) selecting the proper equipment (computer, printer, etc.).

Analysis of these two major problems resulted in the definition of other problem areas that a first time user is faced with. I added Contracts, Scheduling, Machine Familiarization, Software Training, System Testing, Data Conversion and Installation to my list. My next step was to define a logical sequence to present this information, a sequence that would be adaptable to any situation.

Further analysis of these problems led me to the conclusion that a *flow diagram* approach would help me define the steps necessary to achieve the end result—that is, the successful installation of a computer in any small business. Once this flow diagram was completed, I realized I had logically laid down the steps necessary for anyone to take a systematical approach to determining the right programs and computer for their business.

A flow diagram is a simple, step-by-step chart to represent a sequence of actions and activities required to accomplish a specific end result. Suppose you are planning an automobile trip to some distant point. You *chart* or flow diagram the route you will take to reach your desired destination. You plan specific actions along the way, places you wish to stop and rest or visit. Along the way you will be required to make some decisions: turn right, turn left, proceed straight ahead, does the car need gas, am I ready to eat, am I ready to stop for the night, etc. All these actions and activities could be put on paper in the form of a *flow diagram*. You could go to whatever detail you desire. For example, if the decision is to stop for gas you could include in your flow diagram the activities to check the oil level, check the tire pressure, check the radiator, wash the windows, empty the trash, etc.

In the pages that follow I have defined six simple flow diagram symbols I used in my flow diagram. Following these definitions I have reproduced the entire flow diagram. It will be the basis for the logical approach to determining the need for automation and the necessary steps required to assure that the correct decisions are made in the acquisition of both the computer and programs. This flow diagram will show the exact steps necessary to accomplish our objectives.

The Symbols

First, a definition of the symbols that are used in the flow diagram is appropriate. The first is a *Processing* symbol, which will represent any action to be taken by you, the user. As an example, it may mean the definition of your own individual requirements. The processing symbol looks like this:

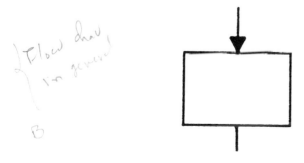

Figure 1-1. Processing Symbol.

The next symbol used in the flow diagram is called a *Decision symbol.* This symbol, when encountered, will indicate a required decision by you before proceeding. There are always two exits from the decision symbol, either a "yes" or "no" alternative for you. However, you alone must determine which branch you will take. The decision symbol looks like the following:

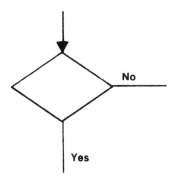

Figure 1-2. Decision Symbol.

The next symbol will be used to indicate a *Predefined Process* or action to be taken by you. An example of this would be to *contact hardware manufacturer.* The symbol looks like:

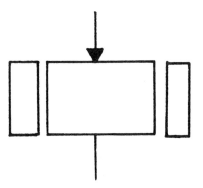

Figure 1-3. Predefined Process Symbol.

The final three symbols, illustrated, are very simple. They are: an *Offpage Connector,* used to designate entry to or from a given page; a *Flow Direction* symbol to indicate the direction or flow; and the *Terminal* symbol, which will signify the completion of all processing steps.

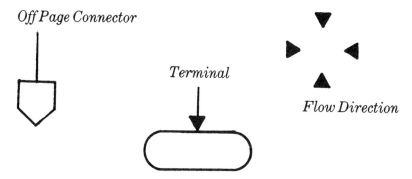

Figure 1-4. Three Flow Direction Symbols.

Do not be concerned that the flow diagram will be like a complex set of blueprints. I have made every attempt to keep it as simple and straight-forward as possible. The flow will indicate the steps that you will be taking to reach your objective, i.e., the successful installation of a small business computer in your business. I will define the steps and activities for you to accomplish (with the aid of the flow diagram). It will be up to you to complete the activities and some simple forms.

The complete flow diagram is reproduced in the pages that follow, but do not be too concerned with it at this time. Each chapter will deal with the information on the flow in a logical sequence which is defined with the help of the flow diagram.

One final word before beginning. I strongly suggest that you read through the entire book before actually beginning any of the required activities. This will give you a feel for what you will be doing and how it will be accomplished.

Selection procedure flow

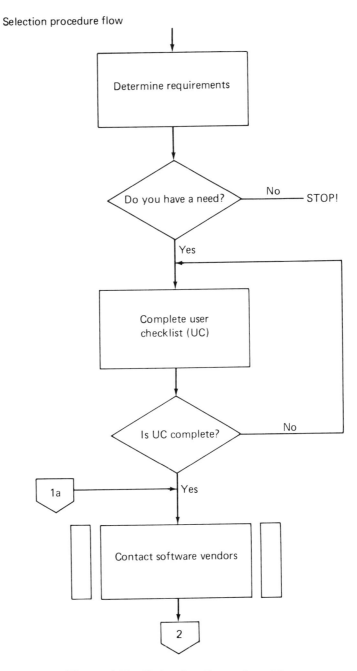

Figure 1-5a. Selection Procedure Flow.

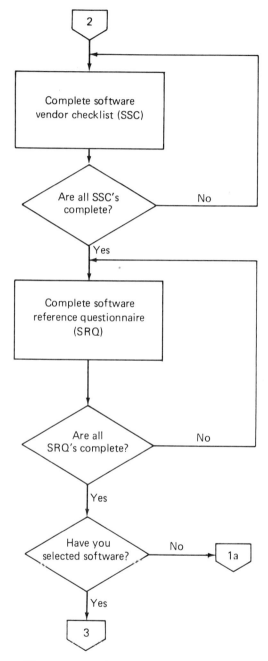

Figure 1-5b. Selection Procedure Flow.

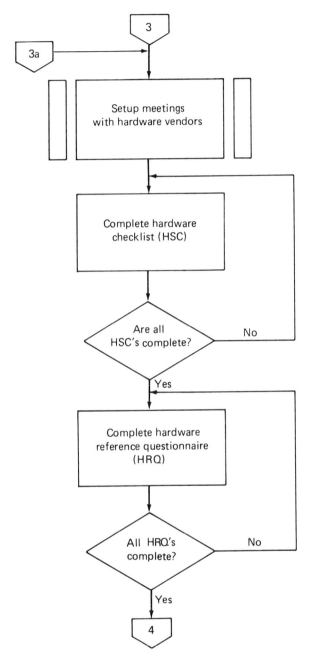

Figure 1-5c. Selection Procedure Flow.

8

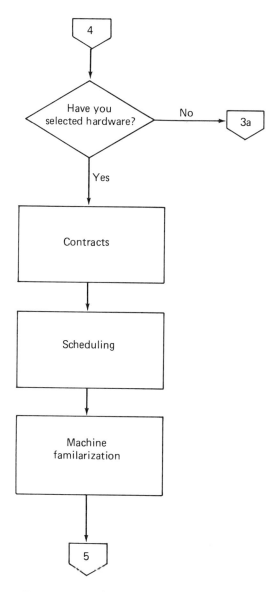

Figure 1-5d. Selection Procedure Flow.

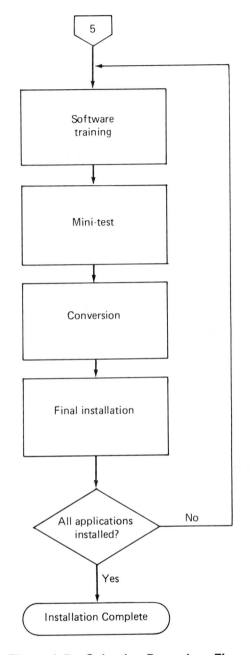

Figure 1-5e. Selection Procedure Flow.

Determine Requirements

Analyzing Your Own Business to Determine the Areas of Application and the Associated Requirements

In this chapter I will outline the procedures for you to use in determining your real computer needs. Various business application areas will be introduced and questions posed. These questions are provided to get you to think about your own business needs. You will undoubtedly think of additional questions that concern you and your own business. The Wish List, Application Worksheet and Requirements Worksheet are introduced in this chapter. The importance of determining business volumes are also discussed.

This chapter is probably the most important chapter in the entire book. If you fail to take the time to define your requirements completely your search for a computer solution will result in frustration and a vast amount of wasted time and effort.

During the last two and a half years, I have installed and assisted in the installation of over 200 applications in small business concerns, ranging from sole proprietorships to corporations employing over 200 people. The majority, however, employed from five to twenty people. Probably the biggest single problem I encountered was identifying exactly what the potential buyer wanted. Even after long hours of discussing needs and requirements, there were always things cropping up weeks and months later that were overlooked at the onset but which were very important to the business. No amount of questioning by a salesman can determine your needs and requirements if you don't know what you really want or need. That's what this chapter is all about—assisting you in analyzing your business and determining what your real needs are. Some forms are contained in the appendices to assist you in determining your *real* needs and requirements. They will be introduced within the text as we proceed.

Determining Requirements

The process of determining requirements is one that you and your staff should accomplish on your own. It is a process in which you analyze your own business and determine those areas where you need accurate, up-to-date information to conduct your business, and the time required to accumulate this information is costly. If you send out 500 statements a month, and it takes your personnel a couple of days each month to accomplish this, you probably have a requirement that can be filled by a computer. If you feel you have lost control in knowing when to re-order inventory items, you probably have a requirement for an Inventory Control system. The prices of your inventory items may be changing so fast that you need an automated method to keep up-to-date in this area. You are really the best judge of what you need and where you need it the most.

The Wish List

To assist you in determining your actual needs, I have designed a simple form (Appendix I) which I call *My Wish List*. On it you will list all those things you wish a computer could do if you had one. Don't be concerned at this point with the column heading Area; it will be dealt with later. To help you get started, I have listed a number of things most small businesses find appealing regarding a computer. If it applies to you, note it on your Wish List.

Inventory Control

- Do you have a large inventory that is critical to the way you do business? Do you wish you knew when a particular item went below pre-established limits?

- Do your inventory costs and retail prices change so rapidly that you are having a hard time keeping up with them? Do you wish you had a system that automatically recalculated your costs when new inventory items were received? Would you like to be able to enter the new list price as you are entering your inventory receipts?

- Do you sometimes wonder how many inventory items you actually have? What they cost you? What your current percentage of markup is? Where they are located? Do you have enough on hand to meet your needs for the next month, or do you have more than you need? A number of wishes can be determined from these questions. Add them to your wish list if they apply.

- Do you wish you had a system to create purchase orders from current inventory counts, established minimums and maximums?

- Do you wish you had a system to determine production requirements based on current orders and future projected orders based on last year's quantity figures, thus allowing you to enter a percentage growth figure?

2. Accounts Receivable

- Do you wish you could begin to charge interest on only those customers thirty days or more overdue?

- Do you wish you could put a reminder on your statements to those overdue and an advertising message on those that are current?

- Do you wish you could know your current Accounts Receivable at any time of the day, without having someone take the time to figure it out?

- Do you wish you could rapidly create a set of labels for all your customers? In zip code sequence?

- Do you have a large Accounts Receiveable, and is it taking longer each month to get your statements out? Do you wish you could get them out faster?

3. Accounts Payable

- Do you wish you knew how much you owed your supplier, when due, if there was a discount available, and how much?

- Would you like to know from whom you purchased the most last year? Could you get a quantity discount if you knew?

- Do you wish you knew how much you needed in the bank next week to pay bills?

4. General Ledger

- Do you spend weekends and nights collecting information for your accountant so he can prepare a current balance sheet? Would you like to have it available at your convenience?

- Does it take you and your staff days to prepare the information for your tax accountant? Does it then take weeks, sometimes months, to get your profit-and-loss statement back? Would you like to get it every day if you needed it?

5. Job Costing

- Do you wish you could quickly and accurately create a bid on an important job using current supply costs, project these costs over a two-year term with a one-percent increase per month, add your own factor for profit, and have a bid prepared for you?

- Do you wish you could accurately and quickly combine your labor costs and materials cost to determine actual job costs?

6. Payroll

- Do you wish it didn't take your staff half a day each week to get your employee checks computed and written?

- Do you wish you could complete your Quarterly Payroll Report quickly and accurately?

- Do you wish you could get your year-end W-2's out as soon as possible?

7. Sales Analysis

- If your profit is down although your sales and volume are up, would you like to know why?

These are just some of the types of questions you should ask yourself. An entire book could be written on just the questions alone.

As you think about your own business, start listing your wishes on the Wish List provided in Appendix I. If need be, ask your trusted employee(s) what their wishes would be if they had a computer to help them in their areas of responsibility.

8. Application Areas

Continue filling out sheets until you feel you have listed all those things you would want a computer to do it you had one. Now let's take a look at the heading on the Wish List called, Area.

Everything you have listed is in essence a *system requirement*. What you have done is to establish your own personal business system requirements. Right now they are all jumbled up since you simply listed everything you would want your new computer to do under ideal conditions. Let's now proceed to define the Application Areas of your requirements. The bottom portion of Appendix II shows a sample list of standard application areas. Using this list and your wish list, begin to identify your requirements, placing them in appropriate application areas. Simply use the abbreviated application reference (Example: Accounts Receivable would be listed simply as A/R).

If you find you have a requirement that doesn't fit any of the sample applications, simply define your own. I will use an example to illustrate the use of the Wish List.

Joe Entrepreneur

Allow me to introduce Joe Entrepreneur, who will help us illustrate the use of each of the forms in this chapter. First, let's get to know Joe a little better.

Joe started his own business a few years ago as a distributor for a national sunglass manufacturing firm. Joe traveled throughout Colorado contacting drug stores, grocery stores, and various small gift shops (selling sunglasses wholesale). He had arranged with a national distributor to get the glasses at below wholesale prices based on the services he would provide. Joe did the entire job, from setting up the display to keeping it well stocked on a regular basis.

Here's how Joe's business was set up. The initial display case and contents were provided at no cost to the business he was supplying. At regular intervals, Joe would return to the store and restock the display, at which time the owner would acknowledge receipt of new merchandise by signing a receipt form. Joe would then bill the owner at a later date (normally a few days later), giving the owner up to thirty days to pay his bill. Joe carried only four grades of sunglasses and therefore had only four inventory items and only four sets of wholesale and retail prices to monitor. On his regular rounds, Joe also handled any merchandise that was returned due to defect, crediting the owner for any merchandise that was returned.

Joe's sales appproach, service, and personality soon resulted in more business than he could handle alone efficiently. So he hired some salesmen and agreed to pay them on a commission basis for their individual efforts in servicing existing accounts and acquiring new ones. Each salesman's commissions were determined by the number and type of glasses sold. Joe also set up a monthly bonus schedule based on volume.

Over the last three years, Joe's business has continued to grow and prosper, and today he employs an office staff of three and a sales force of twenty. But, Joe has problems! When he began his business, it was relatively easy to keep track of the sales for each salesman. Determining the items sold, to whom they were sold, any returned merchandise, and monthly commissions involved only a little extra work once in a while. He now finds himself working weekends and two to three extra hours every night. And somehow he just doesn't seem to be keeping on top of things like he used to.

Joe talked with a friend the other day who bought one of those new small business computers, and things seem to be going well for his friend. So, Joe has decided to investigate the possibility of automating the most critical areas of his business. A hypothetical example? Yes, of course. But let's proceed with an analysis of Joe's problems.

The first thing Joe did was sit down with his office staff and discuss with them the need for automation and solicited their views about the areas that were causing the biggest headaches. The Wish List that Joe and his staff completed is reproduced in Example 2-1.

As you can see, Joe's major problems are keeping track of the sales by his salesmen and calculating commission and bonuses. As his sales force continues to grow, these problems will also continue to take more and more time. Notice that Joe also identified a specific application area for each wish.

If you should find it difficult to determine a specific area, simply assign it to the area you think it logically fits. If you should inadvertently put in the wrong area, don't worry about it. The important point is that you have identified it.

Again, it is very difficult for a computer or software vendor to determine the major problem areas for you without a thorough analysis of your business. Such an analysis by the salesman, if done correctly, could cost you as much as two thousand dollars. Instead, I am attempting to guide you in your own business analysis.

We are now ready to review your wish list and prioritize the application areas in order of importance based on your own business operations.

The Application Worksheet

After completing your wish list, it is important for you to prioritize those areas that you would want to tackle first. In Appendix II you will find an *Application Worksheet*. Simply transcribe the Areas (in priority sequence) to this worksheet.

When Joe completed this function, his *Application Worksheet* listed Sales Analysis first, followed by Accounts Receivable, then Payroll, and finally, Inventory Control. Example 2-2 shows Joe's completed Application Worksheet.

Once you've completed the *Application Worksheet*, you are ready to complete the *Requirements Worksheet* (Appendix III). You may question the necessity of the first two steps. In other words, why can't you just jump to this step and skip the first two? It has been my experience that it works better to simply jot down the problem areas regardless of what area they fall

EXAMPLE 2 – 1

MY WISH LIST

FOR: *J. E. Distributors*

WISH	AREA
1. A method of keeping track of the number and type of sunglasses sold by each salesman	SA/A
2. Availability on a weekly or daily basis of each salesman's total sales for the month	SA/A
3. A quick + easy method of keeping track of the type, latest cost, quantity on hand, quantity on order, + current list price of each of the sunglasses.	I/c
4. A simplified method of entering daily sales, keeping track of who sold them, to whom they were sold, and having a statement printed.	A/R
5. As daily tickets are entered, keep track of the sales for computing commissions and bonuses.	P
6. A rapid method for computing and printing checks.	P
7. The ability to know if a customer is overdue, how long and by how much.	A/R
8. A list, on a weekly basis, of the date a salesman last saw a customer.	A/R
9. Ability to automatically print statements once a month.	A/R
10. Total daily sales (dollars and quantities) by item sold.	I/c

into or whether they are really important at the time. This gives you a comprehensive list of those items that you, and your employees, have determined that you wish you could have. Some of them may prove to be impractical later and therefore not really requirements.

The Requirements Worksheet

When completing the *Requirements Worksheet*, list the requirements in priority order—another reason for completing the Wish List first. This step will become very important at a later time when you are discussing your

EXAMPLE 2 – 2

APPLICATION WORKSHEET

FOR: *J. E. Distributors*

APPLICATION AREAS*

1. *Sales Analysis*
2. *Accounts Receivable*
3. *Payroll*
4. *Inventory Control*
5. _____
6. _____
7. _____
8. _____

* Listed in order of priority.

SAMPLE APPLICATION AREAS

Accounts Receivable (A/R)
Invoicing (I)
Purchase Order Processing (POP)
Payroll (PAY)
Property Management (PM)
Mailing Label System (MLS)
Credit Union Accounting (CUA)
Client Writeup (CW)
Corporate Accounting (CA)

General Ledger (G/L)
Billing (B)
Inventory Control (IC)
Sales Analysis-A/R (SA/A)
Sales Analysis-IC (SA/I)
Job Costing (JC)
Distribution (D)
Partnership Accounting (PA)

EXAMPLE 2 – 3

REQUIREMENTS WORKSHEET

APPLICATION: _Sales Analysis_

FOR: _J. E. Distributors_
PRIORITY: _1_

REQUIREMENTS:

1. A method of keeping track of the number and type of sunglasses sold by each salesman.

2. Availability on a weekly basis or daily basis of each salesman's total sales for the month.

VOLUMES:

Number of Salesman – 20
Number of Tickets per Day per Salesman – 22

requirements with the software salesman. For instance, if you have a requirement listed as a number one priority, and it is not available as part of his package, you may have to look elsewhere.

Our friend Joe completed only three Requirement Worksheets. After some consideration was given to Inventory, he determined that the amount of time spent on keeping track of quantities in Inventory would not be critical if

EXAMPLE 2 – 4

REQUIREMENTS WORKSHEET

APPLICATION: *Accounts Receivable*   FOR: *J. E. Distributors*

PRIORITY: *2*

REQUIREMENTS:

1. A simplified method of keeping track of daily sales, who sold what, who they were sold to, and having an invoice printed.

2. The ability to know if a customer is overdue, how long and by how much.

3. A list on a weekly basis of the date a salesman last saw a customer.

4. Total daily sales (dollars & quantities) by item

5. Automatic printing of statements once a month.

VOLUMES:

Number of Customers – 1250

Daily tickets – 450

Invoices sent (daily) – 450

Monthly Statements Sent – 1100 average

the Accounts Receivable area could provide a daily total based on sales tickets. So, Joe added another requirement to his Requirement List in the Accounts Receivable area. Joe's completed requirements worksheets are shown in Examples 2-3 through 2-5.

EXAMPLE 2 – 5

REQUIREMENTS WORKSHEET

APPLICATION: *Payroll*

FOR: *J. E. Distributors*

PRIORITY: *3*

REQUIREMENTS:

1. As daily tickets are entered, keep track of sales for computing commissions and bonuses.

2. A rapid method for computing and printing checks.

VOLUMES:

20 employees (commissioned & bonus) paid once a month.

3 salaried employees paid weekly.

Determining Volumes

Notice that, at the bottom of the Requirements Worksheet, I have left space for entering various volume figures. In Joe's examples, they have been completed. A brief discussion of what to put here is appropriate at this time.

When I was actively engaged in installing systems in small businesses, I was appalled at their lack of knowledge concerning how many accounts they billed each month. Very few knew. The response was generally, "Oh, about 250, I guess." Well, guessing isn't good enough. More than once I was bitten because the figures were anywhere from 200 to 500 percent off! Small business systems are just that—small! Therefore, you or one of your employees should determine your volumes as best you can, as it is critical for both the hardware salesman and the software supplier to know the *real* numbers. I can think of a few accounts that were not very happy when they found out their new computer did not have the storage capacity to accommodate their volumes. The data you collect is stored on peripheral devices such as floppy diskettes, tapes or hard disks. These devices have limits to the amount of data (information) that they can contain. Be sure the device you select is able to store your collected data.

You should know how many statements you mail out each month. If you have an open-item accounts receivable system (invoices are retained in the computer until paid), it is important to know your average monthly number of invoices. If you have a *balance-forward* type, the transactions are removed at month end. You should know how many suppliers you deal with and add those to the number of regular bills you pay each month. How many employees do you have? How are they paid—weekly, monthly, bimonthly, biweekly? Are they salaried, commission only, hourly, by piecework, or a mixture of all the above? Do you know how many inventory items you have?

Not only are the present figures important, but you should also know if they are increasing. If you purchase a computer today, can you be assured it will be big enough for you in the future?

In completing the Volume section, simply enter everything you can think of that would affect, or could affect storage capacities.

Decision Point "One"

You have finally arrived at the first decision point in determining if you need a small business computer. If you've completed your homework and filled out your Wish List, Application Worksheet, and the Requirements Worksheet, you're to be congratulated on a job well done. Armed with this information, you must now make a decision concerning whether to proceed in your quest for that right computer and the appropriate software. Be sure you have throughly analyzed your business needs. Don't feel you have to make an immediate decision. Take your time. The more thorough you are in determining your requirements the better your chances for success.

As part of this decision-making process, you might consider using a local service bureau as an alternative. If your only requirement is in the area of billing, you might find the service bureau a solution that you can afford without having to install your own computer. You might also find that hiring of additional personnel would suffice. Perhaps your only requirement is the use of part-time personnel during the billing period.

Computers do have their good points and their bad. When they don't work they are useless. They can be exasperating to the highest limits when things aren't going well. However, they don't get sick, take a vacation, or talk back (sometimes). So, make your decision based on what you now know.

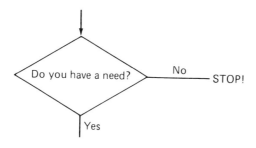

Proceed to Chapter 3

CHAPTER 3

Complete User Checklist (UC)
The Questions You Must Ask—And Answer Yourself!

So, you've taken that critical first step and made the decision to proceed in your quest for the right computer system for you. In this section we will be dealing with you and the things you must analyze besides your need. There are a number of other things you must determine for yourself before even starting to think about computers and programs.

In this chapter we will be using the *User Checklist* contained in Appendix IV. It is your master checklist to determine if you have covered all of your own bases. Each item on this checklist will be discussed in the pages that follow. It is important that you complete this step and make that all-important commitment. Without that commitment by you, your success will be diminished proportionately.

The *User Checklist* contains a number of questions for you to answer. There are three columns: a N/A (not applicable), a N if your answer is no, and a column for Y if your answer is yes. The questions have been designed such that you should come up with a majority of yes answers. If a question does not apply to you, simply enter a check mark under the "not applicable" (N/A) column.

Have You Determined the Need?

Obviously, you should not be at this point if you have not completed the steps outlined in Chapter II. However, it is one of the most important items that should be included on your checklist. If you can't mark your answer under the yes column, you are probably reading this book for the fun of it.

Have You Completed the Requirements Worksheet?

You should have also completed this as part of Chapter 2. If you should come up with other ideas or requirements for a specific area, do not be afraid to go back and add to the Requirements Worksheet.

Don't be embarrassed to put down anything that you feel you might need. If it's something you'd like to see in your new system, add it. Later, your software supplier will let you know if it is available or not.

Have You Prioritized Your Application Areas?

Although this is another item which was covered in Chapter 2, it is worthy of a repeat here. You must know which of your applications are the most important.

Have You Determined Your Business Volumes?

The volume question was covered in detail in Chapter 2. It may have been necessary for you to assign an employee to obtain the necessary figures for you. It is repeated simply because it should be part of your own checklist. You should have everything completed on your checklist before you talk to the hardware salesman and/or the software supplier.

Have You Determined Computer Location?

Determining where you plan to locate your new computer may seem to be a rather moot point. However, I can personally attest to the fact that this item gets little or no attention from the first-time user. There are a number of factors to consider in deciding where to locate your new computer.

Electricity—Most of the new small business computers operate on normal household current (110). However, you should have a separate circuit specifically for your computer, and the associated breaker should be labeled as such. The worst thing that can, and does, happen is that an employee inadvertently throws a breaker not knowing that you are in the middle of some important job on your computer. Clearly label your circuit breaker.

Space Considerations—The new business computers take up very little room. However, if you plan to locate the computer away from the hub of activity (a good idea), you may want to build a partition or possibly a new room. You should have this completed *before* the computer arrives, not after. Since your new computer will play a valuable role in your business, it should *not* be stuck off in a dingy corner because that is the only space available.

Dust Consideration—Of all the various things that can adversely affect a computer, dust is the major culprit. Therefore, the spot you select for your computer should be as dust-free as possible. Locate it away from shop areas and other dust-causing environments.

Carpeting—In some of the dryer states, static electricity can build up in the carpet. Touching the computer and getting a shock, while not critical to you or the computer, can be very annoying. If you're going to install new carpet, you might as well get the non-static type.

Sunlight—Location of the computer away from the direct glare of sunlight should also be a consideration. It's like trying to watch TV with the sun glaring on the screen. We've all experienced what that is like. Locate the computer where the direct effects of bright light or sunlight will not be a factor.

Phone Location—On the first page of one software supplier's document was following: "If you don't have a phone located by your computer, please make arrangements to do so immediately." That ought to tell you something! There will come a time when you will either need to talk to a service person or to a programmer, who may tell you to do something or explain what's happening. Having to run back and forth from the phone to the computer, or having someone yell at you from across the room will simply add to your frustration and impede the progress of your service representative.

High Traffic Areas—Locating your computer away from normal business traffic areas is also very important, the only exception being if you are using it (the computer) for order entry. There are a couple of valid reasons to isolate your computer somewhat:

1)   the information you may be entering, or looking up, may be of such a nature that you'd rather not have it viewed by your customers or every passer-by.

2)   these new-fangled computers seem to attract people, be they "experts"

or friends. I know from bitter experience that you can't operate a computer and carry on a conversation at the same time. The result is almost always disastrous. So, choose a location that is pleasant and *away* from unnecessary interruptions.

Who Will Be Responsible for Your New Computer?

Have you talked to your own employees concerning the idea of automating certain areas of your business? Their reaction is a critical factor. Were they enthusiastic, or did they express fear or mistrust of all computers?

Are you going to operate the computer yourself or do you have an employee in mind? Selection of the right employee is essential to the successful installation of any computer system.

Overall, younger employees adapt more quickly to computers than do the older ones. Our young people have grown up with the idea of computers and some even had some limited experience in either programming or operating one. Somehow they do not seem to have that initial fear that the older employees sometimes do. There are, however, exceptions! I have also seen individuals so afraid of the computer that I seriously felt that they would become physically ill if forced to run the computer.

In selecting the employee whose responsibility it will be to learn the computer and the software system, it is mandatory that some serious thought be given to his or her primary area of responsibility. If you assign your most valued employee the additional responsibility of the new computer, learning to understand the software system, completing the conversion, and daily operation of the system while continuing his or her daily duties, you will most likely meet with failure in your attempt to automate and risk the possibility of losing a valued employee.

Let no one kid you! The process involved in automating your business is not simple. You bought this book for a purpose—hopefully to save you time, money, and a lot of headaches. If it is to be truly useful to you, then you *must* realize that I speak from years of experience in assisting people just like you. I always told my clients "If you listen to me and follow my advice, we can have a good time and get the job done with the least amount of problems and delays." There were those who did and those who didn't. One client took 18 months to automate his business. His most valued employee was the one with the responsibility for everything. Another client had *five* separate businesses up and running in as many months! The difference? He did it all himself and then trained his employees. If you haven't realized it by now, this is the *key to success*! When the boss gets actively involved in the entire process, you can almost always be assured of success.

If You Choose an Employee, Have You Talked to Him/Her?

If you elect to have an employee operate the computer, it would be wise to discuss it with him or her in advance. You may find out that the employee you have selected is going on a vacation when you have your computer scheduled to arrive or has some other conflict of which you are unaware. Will the employee be available for any overtime or weekend work if necessary? In other words, if you do select an employee, don't assume that he or she will be "tickled pink" or have the extra time available that you may need.

Explain to this employee that there may be some overtime required to get things set up and rolling but that in the long run the computer will *save* time. You may want to offer some non-vacation time off after everything is up and running.

The employee you select should have a good grasp for the business world as a whole and of your operation in particular. Knowing how a business is run will be extremely beneficial in adapting the computer to your business or vice versa.

Have You Determined the Best Time to Acquire Your New Computer?

You should choose the time of year which best meets *your* needs rather than those of the hardware or software salesman. You should consider your business cycles, vacations, and holidays. The time frame from Thanksgiving through January 1st is probably the worst possible time. Frankly, I'm surprised at the number of businesses that don't recognize this fact of life. Everyone seems to have their minds on turkeys, Christmas presents, and general holiday get-togethers. If you plan to be up and running before the first of the year, I would suggest you move your schedule back and shoot for the first of November.

Since there probably won't be a perfect time, pick your best time, based on your own personal commitments and those of your employees. Over the years, I have found the ideal time to be mid-January through mid-April. However, any time can be all right, provided everyone is prepared and nothing out of the ordinary comes up.

You might consider hiring additional help during the initial phases. This would include becoming familiar with the computer system, converting the data, and running a mini-test (see Chapter 12). After everything is up and running smoothly, you should be able to cut back.

Do You Want a System That Will Handle Multi-Businesses?

One of the questions you should ask yourself is if you want a software system that you can use for more than one business. Some software companies might help you with the first one, but leave you on your own from there on. Some may set up for one business only. Will you want to tie more than one business together for accounting purposes? You should answer this question yourself before talking to any software supplier.

Are You Willing to Change Your Way of Doing Certain Things?

In most cases, Accounts Receivable means the same thing to all businesses. You have a set of customers to whom you sell services or merchandise, and you bill them each month. Programmers write A/R systems to solve a basic set of accounts receivable problems. These systems are written as generally as possible. You can save money if you are willing to go along with a base system that will handle the majority of your needs. If you want a system tailored to your specific details, you should be ready to pay for that privilege. If you want to be unique, you must also be willing to pay the price. The same holds true for all the other application areas.

Have You Made the Commitment?

This is probably the most important question in this chapter! And, it rests squarely on your shoulders! Without this personal commitment, the road to full automation will be long and difficult. After all your analysis is complete, you must be willing to commit both time and money. Of the two, your commitment of your time will be the most important factor if you are to achieve successful results. If you make only a half-hearted commitment, don't expect that everything will somehow turn out just fine. You have to be prepared to see it through to the end.

If you've made the commitment, then you are ready to take the *yes* path on the flow diagram.

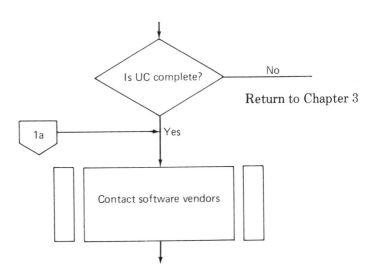

Proceed to Chapter 4

CHAPTER 4

Complete Software
Vendor Checklist (SSC)

*The Questions You Should Ask Your Software Supplier
—and Why You Should!*

Selection of appropriate software to meet your needs is probably one of the most critical decisions you will have to make in automating your business. All kinds of packages are available to handle specific businesses. Some of these can be had relatively inexpensively while others can and do become quite expensive. There is, of course, a vast difference in what you get.

You can shop around for these packages, be they available at a computer store, through the mail, or through a *third party*. You are the *first party*, the hardware supplier is the *second party*, and the software supplier is the third party. In some cases the hardware supplier is both the second and third party.

If you have special requirements and need an existing package modified, you will most likely be dealing with a third party. These third parties can vary from a lone individual to a large company employing many individuals. There are advantages and disadvantages to both.

The sole individual, or a small group of individuals providing software tailoring, will probably be more inclined to work with you at your business location. The modifications you require will get more immediate attention and will more likely turn out the way you want them, and in a shorter period of time. The largest drawback in using these firms is that the attrition rate is extremely high.

With the larger established firms you have the security that they will most likely be around for awhile. One disadvantage in using these larger firms is that they probably won't provide the on-site assistance that you might need. Moreover, modifications will cost more and take longer to get installed. In the end, you have a greater chance of not getting what you really wanted.

This chapter deals with the questions you should ask your software supplier.

In Appendix VII you will find the Software Supplier Checklist (SSC), with three columns for appropriate answers to the questions. In some cases, the question may not apply. If a question is nonapplicable to you, simply check the N/A column. These questions are designed to allow you to probe the company or individual you may be dealing with. It is important to your success that you make a wise choice in the selection of your software supplier. The paragraphs that follow will expand on the questions, giving, when necessary, the reasons for the questions.

Does Their Software Meet Your Requirements?

This is where you can use the Requirements Worksheet developed in Chapter 3. Knowing what you need will help you as well as the software supplier. With your requirements carefully defined, you can determine if the supplier can meet your needs.

Do They Have a Multi-Business Capability?

This could be an important consideration, if you have a number of small businesses that you want to keep separate. If you want to tie them together under one profit and loss statement, it is a necessary requirement for you. You may be able to run the separate businesses but not have the capability of tying them together.

Do They Provide Simply a Base Package?

The majority of the packages that you will encounter can be categorized as *base packages*. They are written by programmers to fill a wide variety of business needs but not specific industry requirements. There are also *special packages* that address a specific industry. Though base packages are, for the most part, designed to fulfill at least 80 percent of the general business needs, the other 20 percent is often the most important to your business needs.

Are Individual Package Pieces Available?

It is not uncommon for a business to buy an entire system (including General Ledger, Accounts Payable, Accounts Receivable, Inventory Control, and Payroll) when it actually needs Inventory Control and Accounts Receivable. That is one of the prime reasons for establishing and defining your needs in Chapter 2. If you don't need all the rest, don't allow yourself to be convinced that you do.

Will They Modify Their Package?

Wholesale modifications can mean the scrapping of entire programmed areas and rewriting them. As a potential user, if you request special modifications that are beyond the scope of the original program, you are asking for trouble. You will end up field testing a new product (program). If, however, you stick with the programs which have been provided, you can normally be assured that they have previously been field tested and all associated problems solved.

Have You Determined the Requirements of the Modifications?

If you do require some modifications to a package, and if the supplier has agreed to make them for you, it is important for you to convey to him exactly what you need. It is equally important that he understands what you want. If it is a new report, you should have him lay it out for you, including the report headings, the sequence in which items are to be printed, and any sub-totals or final totals that you require.

Is There a Separate Contract for Modifications?

Both you and your third party will benefit from having a separate contract for any desired modifications for which a price has been established. While the base contract covers the base system and what you can expect for the price you pay, a separate contract for modifications delineates also what the programmer is expected to do. This will be covered in greater detail in the chapter on "Executing the Contracts."

Have You Determined a Fixed Cost for the Modifications?

Since you will probably need some modifications to the system you have chosen, you *must* determine what these extra modifications will cost you in terms of time as well as dollars. Naturally, people want to know initially what any additional modifications will cost. To leave the question open is only inviting trouble for both parties.

Have You Determined a Time Frame for Modifications?

If the modifications you need are an important part of your business operation, knowing when you can expect the modifications to be completed can be very critical to you. Though most programmers would rather not be pinned down to specific dates, you should insist on an approximate completion and installation date.

If They Modify the Programs Will They Update the Documentation?

Documentation is probably at the top of the list of the things that programmers do not like to do. If the system has been modified, insist that the associated documentation be modified to correspond to your installed system. I would say that the majority of phone calls a third party gets are due to a lack of adequate documentation. Everyone is human, and we all have our bad days. It is under those circumstances that we forget a little item that we need to know and can't find in the documentation.

Can You Review Their Documentation Before Signing the Contract?

Since the lifeblood of any computer system is its documentation, you should ask to see a sample of the supplier's documentation before committing to anything. Moreover, a brief run-through with your software supplier is not adequate. You should plan to take some time to read through it on your own. The following paragraphs will tell you what to look for.

Is Their Documentation Consistent?

Programmers use certain terms to indicate specific operations. For instance, in a customer entry program, the code letter U could stand for *update*. This is not a problem because you, as a data entry person, would rather key a U each time you want to *update* an account than have to type out the word *update*. However, difficulties occur when a number of programmers develop the system, each one using a different specification method or coding convention for updating a customer's record. For example, assume that the programmer who wrote the Accounts Payable area decided to use the letter C to mean *change*. In the Accounts Receivable area, the programmer decided to use the letter U for *update*. Take it one step further and assume that the programmer who wrote the Inventory Control area decided to use the letter M to mean *modify*. In all cases, the result is the same. Whether you *update, change,* or *modify,* the resulting meaning is the same.

From a data entry standpoint, this can becoming very confusing, since you have to remember what area you are working in to determine what code to use. It's called standardization of terms. Look for it, and be aware of the problems that it can cause.

Is Their Documentation Clear?

One of the prime factors to consider when reviewing documentation is whether or not it is clear. Documentation should be written with *you* in mind, not the programmer. You need to know *how to*, not all the reasons *why* it was written the way it was. We can also include the word "complete" in discussing this question. That is, the documentation should tell you everything you need to know concerning the entire operation. A complete review of the documentation should leave you with no questions concerning the operation of the system. The best manuals are those that are written such that the user (that's you) can install his own software system.

Is There a Guarantee That The System Will Do What the Documentation Says?

To protect you, there *must* be some statement in the contract specifying that the programs will operate as documented. If you take the time to review *all* the documentation, and if this clause is included in the contract, you have done the best possible job you can in determining the most suitable software system for you.

Will They Modify Any Inconsistencies?

It is likely that you will encounter something in the documentation not actually reflected in the system you have. If so, ask the supplier to make the appropriate changes on their own time and at their own expense. What you require *most* in your system and associated documentation is *consistency*.

Is There a Section Devoted to Error Detection and Recovery?

There are normally two or three programs in an application that are really the heart of the application; that is, they do all the posting to files and all the updating. If you have any problems with these programs, you should have a set of restart or recovery instructions. Check the documentation. It should identify these critical programs or procedures and what the recovery procedures are.

Are All Output Reports Defined?

These reports are the end result of all information that is fed into the computer, be they receivable statements, payroll checks, or a sales analysis report. All systems have their reports. It is imperative that you know what each report contains, how it is determined (any calculated figures), and how the report should be used! A report is useless to you if you don't know how to read or use it. Be sure that these are well defined. There should be a sample of the report along with a definition of each item on the report. If the item is calculated by the system, the formula should be listed. Likewise, any subtotals or grand total should also be explained. For instance, if the report has a total for Accounts Receivable, you must know if the amount is posted automatically to your general ledger or if you must make the journal entry yourself.

Is On-Site Training Provided?

If you purchase a package through the mail, from a computer store, or from a large firm in some other part of the country, this question is academic. What you will most likely receive is a couple of diskettes, some manuals, and a letter of thanks. On the other hand, if you elect to use a third party or need to because of your special requirements, you will probably receive some on-site training. If so, plan to clear your calendar on those days that it is available so that you can devote your complete and undivided attention to it.

How Much On-Site Training Will You Get?

This question assumes that you will receive some on-site training. If not, code this question with a N/A and go on to the next one. If it is part of the package deal, you should know how much training you will get. Again, this is a two-way street. If you only get a specific amount of time, like two days, you should schedule your time and that of your staff to be *fully* available to take advantage of it. I've experienced many situations where the constant interruptions from phones and other personnel left no doubt in my mind that the trainee would remember little if anything of what went on during the session. If you find that two days' training is not enough, it could be that the concentration was not as much on the training as it should have been.

If you do receive on-site training, it should be in proportion to the number of *functional areas* you agreed to purchase. Obviously, if you purchase five functional areas, you should receive more training than if you purchase only two functional areas. Another consideration is the complexity of the area. The more complex the area, the more training that is required.

Is Additional Training Available?

I have found that the training function is one of the hardest to predict. While some individuals pick it up very quickly, others just can't seem to grasp it! When you expect it to take you an entire day, you're through in three hours. If you plan only three hours, you're there until 7 p.m. If you only get a specific amount of training time, the employee you select is critical. But, what about unforeseen circumstances that require you to change employees in the middle of training or shortly after it is complete? Will the supplier come back and go through it all over again? You hope you won't need it, but what if you do?

What Will Additional Training Cost?

Most third-party software firms will include some training in the cost of their package. Others may charge extra due to the reasons mentioned above. If training is part of the package cost, you would be wise to inquire into the cost of additional training sessions. As mentioned in an earlier paragraph, if the documentation is good, the basic training should suffice.

Is After-Hours Training Available?

The nature of your business may dictate that the training schedule be conducted after the normal close of business. If you foresee this as a possibility, ask if after-hours training is available. If it is not part of the normal procedure, you should be prepared to pay extra for it. After-hours training can be of great benefit if you have the cooperation of your employee(s). Without phones ringing and other unavoidable interruptions, you can get a lot done. However, the drawbacks can outweigh the advantages. At the end of the day, we are all usually tired and ready to relax, and our mental capacities are not at their peak. If you do elect this avenue, I'd suggest going out and having a light dinner before beginning. It will relax everyone, and your benefits will be much greater than going straight through or sending someone out for hamburgers.

Are System Enhancements and Updates Free?

System enhancements and updates are modifications to the system themselves. In some cases, certain rare circumstances arise which prevent the system from working properly. In other cases it is an improvement to the system that benefits all. What you want to know is if this feature is part of the deal, and if it is free.

Who Installs These Free Enhancements?

If you are going to get these free enhancements, you will probably be the one responsible for installing them. Installing enhancements means making modifications to existing program code, something you may not want to tackle, even if the enhancements are free. The people who document these system changes and enhancements can be as bad as the ones who do the documentation. You are dealing with the programmer! If you have to install them, chances are you won't. If you need it, you're probably better off letting your third party do it, or send them a copy of your system and pay them to do it.

Is the Third Party Local or Do They Have a Local Represenative?

If you've got a local representative, seek their advice. They don't have to live fifty miles away to be an expert. If you have someone locally, by all means check them out and, if possible, use them. If you want to purchase a package from a national firm, you'll want to know if they have a local representative. If not, you'll want to know how far away they are and if they are available to serve your needs.

Is Phone Consultation Available?

Phone consultation is important regardless of where your software supplier is located. If it's a one-man operation, his services will undoubtedly be hampered. Again, much depends on the quality of the documentation and the training. Regardless of these two items, will help be available when you need it?

What Type of Telephone Service and/or Response Can I Expect?

If they do provide telephone consultation services, do they also provide a toll-free number? If you end up with a lot of questions, your phone bill will reflect this, potentially adding a few hundred dollars to the cost of your system. Moreover, will someone be at the other end to help you? You may get an answering service or a secretary and find no help at all. If your question is a critical one, and most are at the time, you will want help immediately, not three or four hours later. The other major question is the availability of service. If you're like most businesses, you may decide to work late or on weekends. Is any service or help available then? Will your third-party supplier give you his home phone number? If you use a small company, you'll probably find that some of the services are available only if you ask. So, ask and be prepared. The final question is if this service is free? If so, for how long is it free? Everything has its time limit. You may find that you get three months' worth of phone calls as part of the package price; after that, there might be a charge. Find out how much.

Do They Have Back-Up Support?

If you use a small company or an individual, find out if they have any back-up support. In other words, if they decide to move or go out of business, are you going to be left without service? Accidents do happen, and businesses do fail. If they do have a back-up, get the name and number and check it out.

Do They Have a "Starter-Pac" of Forms?

Almost all systems use a special form of some kind. You may have invoices, checks, statements, labels, etc. You should know if they provide forms to get you started. Since it can take up to eight weeks to get special forms for your new system, you could be up and running in one-fourth that time, if the third party provides these forms. If they provide these forms, you should stick with the format that they have established if at all possible. If you don't, or can't, you are probably looking at additional costs to reprogram for your special forms.

Are There a Variety of Special Forms From Which to Choose?

If the third party does not provide a "starter-pac," they should at least have a few samples of the forms that you can order to fit the programs they have already written for someone else. Don't try to change them just to be original, unless you are prepared to pay the additional cost. Your third party can also help you find a forms supplier. If you find it necessary to have a new form developed, you should work out the format with your third party. After all, they are the ones who will be responsible for writing the new program to match the form. Find out what this new program will cost you.

Do They Provide Conversion Forms?

Conversion forms are forms that define data elements that go into a file, the order in which they go, and any special characteristics about the data. Inventory conversion forms, for example, would probably list the inventory code first, followed by the inventory item description, etc. In all cases each item listed would tell how long (how many characters or numbers were allowed in the input field) and whether any fields had specific values such as EA meaning EACH or GL meaning GALLON. By having these forms, the information can be prepared away from the computer by a number of people.

Do They Provide Conversion Assistance?

Some third party suppliers will supply you with an individual, or individuals, trained to key data. They can enter data faster than you and I can think about it. Based on your business environment and, of course, the cost, you may want to take advantage of this option if it is available. You should also enlist the assistance of your third party in determining the time it will take to complete the conversion process. The individual who tells you that you can accomplish it in a couple of days, even though you have 2000 inventory items to enter, is not in touch with reality. At that rate, an individual would have to enter one inventory item every 30 seconds for 16 hours. You'll find most of the files you will be generating will take a lot longer than 30 seconds to enter.

What Kind of Maintenance Contracts Do They Provide?

You will usually have several choices here, ranging from none on the one end to a high-cost monthly one on the other. In some cases, it's like paying for insurance—you hope you never need it, but if you do, you're glad you've got it. If your requirements are in the areas of payroll or any other function that deals with the local, state, or federal governments, you will probably be faced with tax rate changes at some time or another. Make sure that the maintenance contract covers these contingencies. It will do you little good to buy a payroll package that works this year but not next year because you have no one to update the tax tables. It might also benefit you to take a monthly maintenance contract for the first six months and then switch to an annual one, if it is available. If you find that the only one available is an annual one, check the cost. You may find that what you get is not worth the cost.

Does Their System Provide for Automatic Back-up Procedures?

Back-ups simply means duplicating your information in case of catastrophe. A good software system should provide an automatic back-up procedure that is simple and easy to use, and it should be a part of a normal daily function. I've found that if you don't force a back-up each day, the user will gradually stop doing it. Then, BANG! Something goes wrong and the programmer or the machine is to blame. Backing up your system every day is like using your car seat belt *all* the time—you hope you never need it, but if you do, you are prepared. Automatic back-up procedures force you to complete the task before you can continue.

Do They Provide or Will They Assist You in Establishing an Implementation Plan?

This plan would help you schedule your time and your employees' time in getting everything up and running. Your third party will know, for instance, if you need to enter your Inventory items before you can use the accounts receivable area. In some instances he may be able to dummy up an inventory file for use with the accounts receivable area while you are organizing and entering your real inventory. There will also be the consideration of the training sessions, the testing, the data conversion, and final installation. The information in this book will give you that guidance if you decide to go it alone.

Have They Provided You With All Contracts?

You should request a copy of all contracts that you will be executing with your third party. They should be completely filled out and specify the additions that you require and the associated costs. I would strongly suggest that you have your attorney review these documents *before* you sign them.

Have You Obtained the Three References?

Just as with the hardware salesman, you should obtain at least three references, regardless of where you obtain your software. The next chapter will deal with the questions you should ask these references. If you're going to be a "guinea pig" (the first one to use the new system), then you should get a definite price break. Since you will be used to field test this new system, you might as well benefit from it in some way.

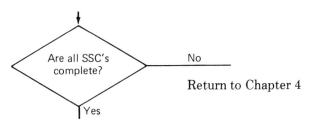

Return to Chapter 4

Proceed to Chapter 5

CHAPTER 5

Complete Software Reference Questionnaire (SRQ)

The Importance of Contacting the Software Vendor
References—Some More Questions

This chapter deals with those names you obtained as references from your prospective software supplier. If the software supplier can give you three names of people he has supplied (and you get a good recommendation from these references), you can be confident in his statements and product.

We will be using the *Software Reference Questionnaire* (SRQ) in this chapter. The questions are designed to elicit confirmation of the information you obtained from the software supplier. You should have no problems getting the answers to your questions. If a customer is happy with his system, he should be pleased to help you; if he is displeased, you'll be the first to know!

These are some more of those questions that have no right answers. What you are looking for is really, "How did it all go?" There are no columns for checking yes or no responses. You are seeking confirmation of the claims made by the software vendor. If he's got three happy customers, that would be good enough for me. The types of questions you should ask are briefly discussed in following paragraphs. Some of the questions and answers you get will cause others to come to mind. These are simply a few to get you started.

What Applications Did You Originally Plan to Install?

This question will allow you to fill in the blank line at the top of the SRQ. What you would really like to find is a reference who has something close to what you need.

Did You Get Installed What You Had Originally Planned?

There can be a lot of reasons why something isn't up and running. Maybe, your reference was simply oversold and didn't have a real need for what is still remaining.

If his or her answer is no, your obvious question would be, "why?" Perhaps they're not far enough along. Perhaps someone quit on him. If that's the case, you'll want to know if it was because of the computer.

Did You Find the System Easy to Learn?

The documentation was discussed in detail in the preceding chapter. Even if the documentation is clear, it takes both the document and the machine (computer) to make a team. They have to be a matched set. The fault might not be with the documentation; rather, it may be that the problem is with the machine. So when asking this question, try to determine if it is the system or the computer or both.

Is the Documentation Consistent With the Programs?

Though the software salesman may have told you it is consistent, get it substantiated from someone who knows and who has worked with the system. You'll want to ask your references if they had any modifications made to the system; if so, was the documentation also updated? Also ask if the changes that were made were consistent with the rest of the system.

How Long Did It Take You to Get Up and Running?

Based on the applications that he installed, you can get an idea of the complexity of his system. Ask him about his business, how many people he employs, how big his inventory is, etc. With this knowledge you can get a feel for the time that will be required to get your system operable.

Did It Take You Longer Than You Were Led to Believe?

You can also ask him if there were any problems that he encountered that he wished he had known about before he started. Most software distributors would like you to believed that it is easy. Well, it is for them—after all, most of them have been working with computers and software for years. What they sometimes don't realize is that many people have both a desperate need for, and at the same time a basic distrust of, computers.

Did the Programs Live up to the Sales Pitch?

Even though all the purchased systems may be up and running, they may haven fallen short of their intended goal. You'd like to know if you can expect to get what you were promised.

What Has Been the Response to Any Problems You Encountered?

If the response from your references is that they have no problems, you're in business. Nine times out of ten times you will find that they had some problem at some time. What you want to know is, "How was the problem handled?" What kind of problem was it, and did it get resolved to their satisfaction?

Are They Knowledgeable in General Business Practices?

It's important, from an analytical standpoint, that your software representative has a good grasp of the general business environment. If they don't, how can they really help you if you have a problem but don't know how to solve it. It also gives one a feeling of security knowing you're working with someone who can relate to your problems and suggest solutions. Check his business sense: is he going to be a help to you if you need it?

Did They Help You With the Conversion?

I've worked with some clients who had to do their inventory conversion over four times to get it right. Possibly I didn't explain it well enough or place enough importance on it. What you'd like to know is if they had similar problems that could have been avoided if a more detailed explanation had been presented. Also, you'd like to know if conversion forms, etc., would have helped to speed up the process.

Did They Work Well With Your Employees?

It's important that the installer or trainer or whatever they call him is kind, considerate, etc. In almost 50 percent of the cases, the individual who will be responsible for the computer will have some fears or misgivings concerning the computer. I always found it very helpful to break the ice, so to speak, by approaching the job as being fun and exciting. You've got to laugh and have fun. If the installer is gruff and treats you like an ignoramus, it's not going to be fun!

Were There Any Hidden Costs?

Hidden costs are those not explained before any contracts were signed, costs you did not anticipate. If you request special changes, you can expect to get charged extra for them. These are not hidden costs. However, getting a charge for a phone consultation three months after installation, if it was never made clear at the beginning, is a hidden cost. Anything that cost your reference money that he never bargained for can be put in this category.

Have They Completed the Job to Your Satisfaction?

That final 10 percent is always the toughest. When you sign up, everything is roses and clover. You have your new machine, and the third party has your money, or at least part of it. Total installation doesn't happen in just a few short days—it takes some time. What you're looking for is a dedicated third party who will see the job through to completion, regardless of whether he loses money or not. Most of them live on their reputation to complete a job— or they die by it. If only one out of three references is dissatisfied, you still probably have a winner to go with.

If You Had It to Do All Over Again, Would You?

This is a big question, one that will reveal a lot about how things really went. If your reference had problems but would still do it all over again, you can be assured that his system was well worth the effort. It may have taken him time and money to get where he is, but he is most likely saving more time and money now than he did before. He probably has more information and a greater capacity for expansion without adding additional employees. The road may be rough, but the rewards should be worth it.

Would It Be Possible to Stop By and See Your System?

This is the final question, and a very important one. You can probably learn more about your reference's business and the type of people who run his computer by taking the time to visit him for a few hours. If he's genuinely proud of his computer, he will probably agree. If he is nearby you may be able to set up an arrangement to use each other's computer if yours, or his, happens to go down for a day or two. It can happen. It would be nice to know you had a back-up system available.

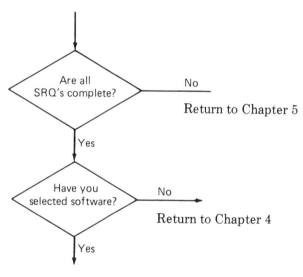

Are all SRQ's complete?

No — Return to Chapter 5

Yes

Have you selected software?

No — Return to Chapter 4

Yes

Proceed to Chapter 6

CHAPTER 6

Complete Hardware Checklist (HSC)

A Detailed Discussion of the Questions You Must Ask Your Hardware Salesman—and Why!

In the old days, computers were big and expensive. Though hardware salesmen spent a lot of time and money wooing prospects, their compensation was well worth the time spent with prospective clients. But times have changed! As the cost and size of computers have reduced, the market has broadened to include businesses one would have thought too small to computerize. However, as the cost and size of the computers came down, so did the salesmen's commissions. Thus, they can no longer afford to spend as much time with a prospect. I mention this fact because you should be aware that after the computer sale has been consummated, the salesman must move on.

Although some companies do sell both the hardware and the software, be prepared to talk to different people. The salesman is a salesman because he's good at it, but he's most likely not a programmer and wouldn't want to be one. The questions in this section are designed to help you become knowledgeable concerning computer hardware. If the hardware salesman can't answer them, have him call someone that can!

The demonstration that you will be shown, whether in your office or at a computer store, will most likely be a canned demonstration which will hit the highlights only. *It's likely that the system you see demonstrated is not even installed anywhere!*

In this chapter, we will be using the Hardware Salesman Checklist (HSC) contained in Appendix V. Each item on this checklist will be discussed in the paragraphs that follow. As with your own checklist, you should come up with as many yes answers as possible. You should fill out one of these for each computer you are interested in, that is, for each hardware salesman you talk to.

Have You Obtained at Least Three References?

It is extremely important that you obtain names of at least three other people you may contact—people who are actually using the computer you are contemplating buying. If there aren't any because the computer is new, try to arrange a discount for testing the product. Without these names, you will have to rely on your own judgment. I would recommend that you get those references or look for another company.

Does the Manufacturer Provide On-Site Maintenance?

The most advantageous situation is one in which the computer manufacturer provides service personnel to come to your location and fix your machine in your office.

Where is the Location of the Hardware Maintenance?

In other words, if something goes wrong with the computer, who do you call and where are they located? Most of the hardware manufacturers of small business computers have a staff of individuals who fix the machine when it is sick (not working). The location of these individuals is very important. If you're going to be using your new computer as an integral part of your business, you can't afford to wait days or weeks to get it repaired. If you have to take your computer in to be fixed or send it away, are you prepared to live with the attending inconvenience, cost, etc.?

Computer Maintenance Cost, Duration, and Availability?

You should ask about the availability of a computer maintenance contract. Is your new machine to be under warranty and for how long? What about after the warranty period? Will maintenance be available? How long will it be made available—one year, five years? What will the maintenance service cost? What did it cost last year? How often does the cost of the maintenance increase? What would the rates be then? What if you don't accept the contract and you need help?

Is There a Replacement Machine Available?

Let's suppose that your machine goes down. The repairman arrives and, after a few hours, he finds the problem. But, he doesn't have the part he needs! He does some checking and finds out this part has been failing and that it will be a couple of days before he can get the necessary replacement part! You explain to him that your computer is an integral part of your business. Will they provide a machine for you to use in the interim?

Will the Computer Handle Your Volumes?

Armed with your research information (Chapter 2), you can ask intelligent questions concerning the capacities of the computer in question. If there is a question concerning this item, enter a "?" beside this question on your checklist.

The volume question has two prongs associated with it. In the first place, is your business activity so large that a small business computer could not handle the volume? The other question is dealt with in the next paragraph, namely that of storage capacities.

Is There Enough Storage Capacity For Your Data?

Volume is an important consideration. However, even if the computer can handle your volume, does it have enough storage capacity to accommodate and retain the necessary daily, monthly, or historical information you need? Small business computers are just that—small! The salesman will have to assist you in answering this question.

Is the Storage Capacity Expandable?

If you need additional storage now or in the future, can you get additional storage devices? Some computer manufacturers have an expandable *storage capacity.* If you need it, or if you think you might need it in the near future, can you get it? How long will it take to get and what will it cost?

Will There Be Hardware Training at Your Office?

You should find out if you're to be left with the computer and a handbook and made to go it alone. In some cases there may be a handbook and a cassette tape. If you find this inadequate, what else is available?

Are There Training Seminars?

In addition to a handbook and a cassette tape, the manufacturer may also provide seminars. If so, where are they held and how much will they cost you?

Have You Reviewed the Training Manuals?

You should ask to see a copy of the training manuals. If the salesman doesn't have any, ask him to send you samples before you decide. Take the time to review them. You should be able to read and understand them. Sometimes these so-called training manuals are written for programmers rather than for the first-time user.

Does the Manufacturer Provide Software?

Most hardware manufacturers provide software for their computers. However, the important question is if it meets your needs and specifications. If you are contemplating using the hardware manufacturer's software, you should be prepared to fill out the Software Supplier Checklist also. The same questions apply regardless of where you get the software.

Does the Computer Require Any Special Wiring?

This question was covered earlier. However, it is a question that should be asked concerning each of the computers you are investigating.

Does the Manufacturer Provide Utilities?

The word *utilities* simply means those miscellaneous functions that allow you to copy files, use disks, edit, etc., as you find necessary. The important point here is that these are very difficult for the first-time user to understand. It's almost a prerequisite that they provide you with some training in addition to the manual that you will receive. Have the salesman go through it with you, step by step.

Is the Computer Upward Compatible?

If you anticipate any further growth in your business, you might want to know where you can go if you outgrow your new computer. The term *upward compatible* means that any program you buy for your computer will run on a larger computer with little or no change. The key is the little or no change phrase. Without upward compatibility, it could cost you in the future if you are anticipating some growth.

Is There a Toll-Free Number to Call for Computer Problems?

This item is related to the service question we covered earlier. If you have problems with your machine, will you have to invest your own funds to contact a service representative? During what hours is a service representative available for on-site maintenance? Is it available after 5 p.m.? What about weekends?

Is There an Error Book and Can I Understand It?

The errors that a computer can come up with fall into two categories. The first deals with the computer and its associated printers and storage devices. The computer will give you an error message if you forget to turn your printer on, or if the printer runs out of paper. These types of errors deal with the computer and are designed to tell you what action you are to take. The second type are those that deal with the computer programs. You should know how to distinguish between the two. In the case of the first type, you may simply have to take some action to correct the situation. The latter case is a little more serious. You should not have errors with the programs. If you do, you should contact your software supplier.

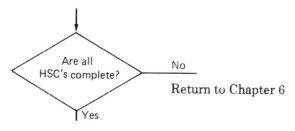

Proceed to Chapter 7

CHAPTER 7

Complete Hardware
Reference Questionnaire
(HRQ)

*The Questions You Should Ask Someone Who Has the
Computer You Are Contemplating Buying!*

This chapter deals with those names that you obtained from the hardware
salesman, be he independent or connected with a computer store. These are
the names of people who have installed the computer you are contemplating
buying. These people can be a wealth of information, as they can tell you a
number of things concerning the computer that you would be unable to discover otherwise. This chapter deals with the type of questions you should
ask, and why. It is not meant to be a totally complete list. I've tried to give you
an idea of the types of questions to ask.

You should not be afraid to ask the kinds of questions that will give you
the information you need to know. After all, you may be planning to expend

thousands of dollars yourself. A few minutes on the phone or a half a day visit could save you those thousands of dollars.

The Hardware Reference Questionnaire (HRQ) is contained in Appendix VI. There are no yes and no columns because these questions have, for the most part, no right answer. You should simply ask the questions and take notes. If any other pertinent questions come to mind, add them to the list. Each one of these questions will be discussed briefly in this chapter in the paragraphs that follow.

How Long Has Your Computer Been in Operation?

This is a very important question. If your reference has only had the computer a few weeks, you should take this into consideration when evaluating his or her answers. An ideal reference would be one whose computer had been installed for a number of months and whose *applications* were similar to yours.

What Applications Does Your Computer Have?

Hopefully, the salesman gave you some reference whose applications are similar to yours. In most instances, this will not be the case. What is important is that you get a feel for the complexity of his or her installed applications. It would be valuable to know if all he or she is running is a simple mailing system, or if the computer is used simply to post journal entries to a set of accounts.

Do You Plan to Add Other Applications?

You never know which of your questions will result in the most valuable information. Just knowing what a user is doing and what is planned for the future may yield information you might not have gained in any other way. If your reference has had a number of problems with the computer applications, you may want to look elsewhere for your hardware.

How Much of the Day Is the Computer Being Used?

If you first know what the computer is being used for, you can then ask how much of the day is spent on the computer. From the answer you can determine if the computer is sufficient for your own volumes. Of course, you need to know how long the computer has been in operation. Since it takes some time to become familiar with the machine, understand the software system, and get a normal office routine set up based on the computer, it's important to know if your reference is still in a *conversion* stage.

Has the Computer Proved Reliable?

What you are trying to determine here is if there have been any significant problems with the hardware itself. If the reference has had to place a number of service calls, it is important to know if the problem was recurring. That is, was the problem fixed the first time, or did it require a number of calls to determine the problem and get it fixed?

Has the Computer Ever Been Completely Down?

You may have problems with a computer of a specific nature and still be able to use certain portions of the hardware. For instance, if the printer is down, you may still be able to perform any operation that does not involve the printer. Being down to me means being totally nonfunctional. It's an important point to consider. If the computer is so sophisticated that any little problem takes the entire system down, you could be in serious trouble if you need one that is up and running all the time.

How Long Did It Take the Maintenance Man to Respond?

You'll have to use some judgment here. If a problem occurred that put the entire computer down, and it took a couple of days for them to get to your reference, I'd want to know why. Hardware service personnel can get a number of service calls in a short period of time. Normally they will call you back as soon as possible and try to determine the nature of your problem. If they have a number of problems at the same time, they will work on the most urgent problem first, then gradually move to the one of the least urgency. If you are using a computer for order entry and your computer is down, it is urgent. If, however, you have a key on your keyboard that sticks occasionally, he will get to you after the more critical problems have been taken care of.

How Far Away Is Your Maintenance Man?

This is good to know. Though one hundred miles might not seem too far away in the month of July, how about during the month of January? If you live in the snowbelt and your repairman is a long way away, you could have a problem. Some hardware manufacturers will guarantee that the service man will be there within a certain time frame. I've always wondered what happens if he's not. Do I get to slap his wrist? *interesting*

Is There Another Machine Close By?

If the individual you are contacting is close by, you can probably arrange to use each other's machines if either one of you is completely down. You might want to broach the subject the first time you talk to a reference, as you could both benefit in the long run.

Has the Repair Service Been Adequate?

Assuming that your reference has had to use it, it is important to know if the service was adequate. If the repairman was rude or inconsiderate for no reason, you won't look forward to working with him if your machine goes down. Sometimes the repairman can make a user feel inadequate, since they operate on a technical level. Just remember, we all have our bad days. Most of them that I've had the pleasure of working with have been both kind and considerate.

Who Operates the Computer?

This is another one of those questions that can relate to a number of the other questions. If the owner took the full responsibility for the computer at the beginning, it is worthy to note. It may mean that his problems would carry more weight than if he is getting his information second hand. Owners of small businesses take more interest in what's happening in their business than does an employee. So, the answers you get to all of the questions carry more weight if the boss is operating, or did initially operate, the computer.

Is the Computer Easy to Learn to Use?

The salesman can tell you it is a snap to learn; but, for whom is it a snap? Him? If he's been in the business for a few years, it probably is. However, will the individual who has had absolutely no exposure to a computer find it as easy? Your reference can tell you a lot. You should also ask if the individual running the computer had any prior experience. The absolute best reference you can get would be one where no one in the office had any prior experience on any computer, and the report you get from them is that it was as "easy as pie."

Who Supplied the Software?

If your reference has any applications similar to your own it will be important for you to know who supplied the software. You can then pull out your software Supplier Reference Checklist and go to work.

Was the Installation Harder Than Expected?

I would add to that the question of whether it was harder than your reference was led to believe? This can lead to many related questions as to what he found the hardest? Why was it difficult? What could have been done by your reference or the hardware supplier to eliminate these problems, or at least to lessen them? You may want to add an item on your list for the hardware salesman that you will buy if certain conditions are met. Maybe it's simply inadequate training on the part of the supplier.

Can You Stop By to See The System in Operation?

This question is sort of a bait question. Based on the reaction you get, you can get a feel for how it is really going. If things have not gone well for him, he may not want to let anyone know the real situation and the reasons behind it. On the other hand, your reference may ask you first to stop by, in which case he's obviously proud of his system and the part he played in getting where he is. By all means, take him up on his offer, as he can be a wealth of information to you.

Have There Been Any Electrical Problems?

As mentioned before, most of the small business computers run off normal household current and are not affected by the normal fluctuations of this current. Though it may be a relatively unimportant question, ask it anyway. You never know what you may find out.

How Would You Rate the Hardware Documentation?

As mentioned earlier, most computer-supplied *documentation* is not written for the end user. The individuals who compile these documents have never been out in the "real world" and worked with an account. There's an old saying that I learned early in the computer profession. It goes, "If you can't write a program, they'll make a program analyst out of you, and if you can't handle that, they will let you write the documentation."

Have There Been Problems With the Computer Location?

Here you can check my statements that I made in an earlier chapter regarding sunlight, dust, and traffic. You might want to know if the computer is located in a separate room or if it is in the midst of normal traffic. If the machine is to be used for order entry or inquiry functions, it will have to be located in the area where it is needed.

What Did You Find Most Difficult About the Computer?

This is the catch-all question. You'd like to know if there is anything at all that you haven't asked that caused a problem. Likewise, you'd like to know if there is anything that you can do to avoid running into the same thing. Again, it may relate to training or it may possibly relate to inadequate preparation on his part.

Conclusion

I've tried to list all the things that come to mind that will help you in finding out all you can concerning a computer that you are contemplating buying. If you think of others, add them to your list. The items listed in this chapter should get you started and point out the necessity for contacting your references.

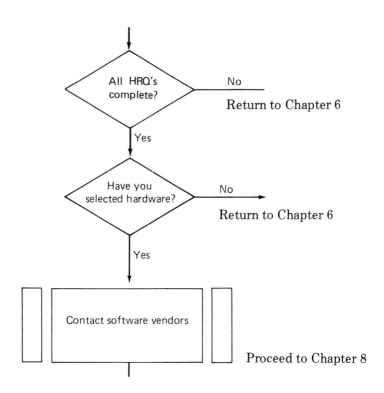

CHAPTER 8

Contracts

Consummating the Deal—What Types of Contracts To Look For—and Why.

You should, of course, consult a competent attorney when dealing with contracts of any kind. What this chapter is all about is the types of contracts that you could encounter based on the direction you choose. If you buy everything from a computer store, you will encounter few contracts. However, if you use the second party (a hardware manufacturer) and a third party (supplier of software systems), you are likely to encounter several.

Computer Purchase Contract

You probably won't find much flexibility in this contract, as it will be a standard one specifying the equipment you are purchasing, the price, the terms, and the conditions. What you should look for is how long the computer is under <u>warranty</u> and what is covered during that time frame. You may have some options such as purchase, lease with purchase option, or simply lease. Depending on your financial position, one may have an immediate advantage over the other. Ask about the various plans available.

Computer Maintenance Contract

This is the insurance policy you can elect to buy once the warranty runs out. A general rule of thumb is <u>one percent per month of the total computer</u> cost. Refer to some of the other chapters concerning the maintenance contracts and the questions you should ask. If a valuable component in your computer fails, the cost of replacing it could equal one-fourth the cost of the computer itself. If that were to happen, you'd be glad you had the service agreement. You should check to see what it covers. If it is one that provides on-site maintenance, find out what hours of the day are covered. I know of one case where a client called the repairman in at twenty minutes to eight in the morning and got charged overtime because the time before eight o'clock was not covered by his maintenance contract.

Software System Purchase

If you purchase your software at a computer store, it will probably just be added to the contract for the computer. These programs will be thoroughly tested and will operate as they were documented 99 percent of the time. The problem with them is that they most likely will not meet your full requirements, and you won't be able to change them.

If you elect to use a third party, you can expect a variety of contracts. The types are probably as numerous as are the third parties. If you can use their programs as is, all the contract has to say is what you are getting and what it will cost.

If you have been told that you will receive three days of training, it should say so in the contract. It should also state if any other services are available after final installation, along with a definition of what final installation or final acceptance means. Avoid those contracts demanding all money initially though the installation is spread out over two or three months. Look also for the clause which allows you to retain a certain percentage of the total price until completely installed. Companies which allow this are normally sure of their package and of themselves.

System Enhancements Contract

If you have enlisted the talents of a third party to do some system tailoring for you, you should request a separate contract for this. This contract should spell out what you will receive and the associated costs. You will probably be asked to advance some money at the time the contract is signed, with the balance due upon installation. If the system modifications are going to provide any new reports or display screen formats, these should be defined, drawn out, and included as part of the contract. Try to get as much defined and included as an attachment to the contract as possible. The bigger the modification, the more detailed the specifications should be.

Software Maintenance Contract

You may wonder why you would need something like this after your system is finally installed and operating.

Based on the type of applications you installed, it may not be necessary. However, if you have payroll as part of your system, you surely want to know that someone is going to be around and obligated to change your tax tables when it becomes necessary.

You may encounter a couple of different types of contracts. One may merely allow an annual contract, while another may have only a monthly contract or possibly both. If you have a monthly one available, you would probably be wise to take advantage of it for a few months.

Once you have accepted the system, the third party is no longer obligated to deal with you concerning any problem you might encounter. They will normally respond for a period of time after installation, but if you have difficulties 12 months later, they may not want to, or have the time available to help you. A maintenance contract would require them to make their services available.

CHAPTER 9

Scheduling

*Arranging For Machine Installation, Training, Testing,
Conversion, and Final Installation*

Scheduling is an art which some people acquire and others don't though it is not really difficult. It simply involves planning a schedule of activities that must happen to achieve a desired result. Many books and papers have been written to assist those who need the help. Some are very complex, while others are relatively easy to understand.

A general misconception is that a schedule is sacred and must be met at all costs. Schedules are not! They are simply tools to use in planning a *series* of events that hopefully will happen as projected. Outside forces may alter plans, but this cannot be predicted in advance. Approach the process of scheduling with the attitude that it is your desire that these activities will happen as planned, and if modifications are necessary due to unforeseen circumstances, you will simply modify your schedule.

The Scheduling Worksheet in Appendix IX is provided to assist you in scheduling the activities necessary to install each software application. Though it is very simple and straightforward, it is discussed briefly in this chapter.

Scheduling Your Own Installation

Probably the first decision you must make is in which sequence you would like to install the applications you have purchased. Your software supplier should assist you in this area. There may be some prerequisites, or a predefined sequence of application installation. If you're doing your own installation, you will have to determine this for yourself. The training item for each application will consist of reading a manual and experimenting with an area until you know it well enough to set up your own test. If you are using a third party, enlist their assistance in the training phase.

Another factor influencing the duration of each scheduled application will be the complexity of the area and/or the amount of data. While in some cases the entire process may be completed in a couple of days, other applications could conceivably take a number of weeks to complete. The important thing to remember is to complete all the required steps (i.e., training, testing, data collection, and final installation).

Your schedule should include any holidays, vacations, or other planned activities. If you are using a third party, they will have to work with your schedule and you with theirs in establishing the times both of you will be available for the training sessions.

Some consideration should also be given to the time of month in which to make the final cutover to the computer. For instance, it would be a good idea to plan to change over to the computer in the Accounts Receivable area immediately after statements had been put out. All the balances would be correct and all the activity reflected on this statement. If the cycle falls on a Friday, all the better. You may want to plan to use Saturday as the day to enter the balances, with the idea of starting the following Monday on the computer.

The scheduled arrival of any required special forms should also be a part of your planning. Allow enough slack time in your schedule for them to be available when you actually need them. You should plan to have them available for your test phase. Don't assume that they will line up! Check them out yourself. If there is a problem, you may have to have a program changed or the forms reprinted.

Some scheduled activities can occur simultaneously depending on how much help you have. For instance, while an employee collects and prepares the data for Inventory, you could be in the final phase on Accounts Payable.

You should, however, fully complete a given application area before attempting to bring up another area in live mode. Trying to do too much at one time could result in problems.

Figure 1 is an example of how the Scheduling Worksheet is used. In the example, only two applications were involved. The month and day lines were filled in after a date had been established for the arrival of the computer. Payroll was the first application to be brought up. As you can see, only a very short period was necessary to bring up the payroll application.

Don't be afraid to use the worksheet to make notes concerning scheduled delivery date of the forms or any other information that you find necessary to add. Some space has been left between the activities to add any other activity—information that you may find necessary to accomplish as part of your application installation.

The only other application that this simple example illustrates is General Ledger. As you can see, the data collection phase for General Ledger was going on at the same time the conversion was going on for payroll. What was most likely happening was that the user was working with his accountant in establishing his set of accounts for the computer. He was also probably arranging to get the required information to feed into the computer during the conversion phase for General Ledger.

Use this example as a guide in scheduling your own installation with the idea that it can be revised if required.

SCHEDULING WORKSHEET

FOR: T. E. Distributors

FUNCTIONS	MONTH	JULY										AUGUST										SEPT					
	DAY																										
Computer Arrives		x																									
Machine Familiarization		→																									
APPLICATION (Payroll)																											
Training				x																							
Test Data Selection					xx																						
Mini Test					xx																						
Review Test						x—x																					
Data Collection							xx																				
Conversion									x																		
Installation																											
APPLICATION (G/L)																											
Training							x—x					x															
Test Data Selection								x—x				x															
Mini Test													x														
Review Test													xx														
Data Collection								x—x							x—x												
Conversion																	x										
Installation																			x								

Figure 9-1.

68

CHAPTER 10

Machine Familiarization

Getting To Know Your Computer

At long last, the decision has been made and the computer has finally arrived. There it sits, all shiny and new. Now what?

In the preceding chapter we discussed the need for setting up a schedule of activities. One of the items listed was machine familiarization. It's really the same thing as getting acquainted with a new electronic watch you bought or any other gadget that comes with a set of instructions.

You should have scheduled sufficient time for yourself and/or the employee you have selected to operate your new computer to get to know this new piece of equipment. You will undoubtedly get a number of manuals with your new computer, and it is imperative that you know what is contained in each and how they should be used. One of them will likely be a self-teaching guide to the programming language that the computer uses. Even if you're not planning to do any programming at this time, you might as well get it out of the way.

What you are interested in are the manuals that you will need to help you get to know your new machine. There will probably be a manual that gets you started, telling you how to turn on the computer and discussing the various functions available on the keyboard. There may also be a pre-programmed routine that the manufacturer supplied to assist you in getting familiar with the computer and the features available. In some cases the manufacturer may provide some samples and/or a games diskette to assist you in getting to know your new computer.

There should be a section in the manual or a separate manual for some functions called *utilities*. These functions, regardless of what they're called, will allow you to copy information (files), sort files, perform specific calculations, etc. Familiarize yourself with this document and the functions that are available.

I have installed some software systems where the computer was never turned on after the computer salesman left. Under those circumstances, I was starting from nothing. The primary reason given for not trying anything was the fear of doing something wrong. Don't let that happen to you! Turn on the machine. Go through the manuals. Learn as much as you can about your new machine on your own. You'll remember it twice as long.

CHAPTER 11

Software Training

Learning Each Application—a Step At a Time!

This step in the application is very important. If you give it little attention, you will find that you are attempting to run a system application that you don't fully understand. It should be your goal to learn as much as you can about the application area. If there are any weak points, now is the best time to discover them, not when you're trying to use the system as an integral part of your daily business.

Review The Application Documentation

Take the time to read through the section in the documentation for the application that you are working with. Try to get as familiar with it as you possibly can. If there are terms that you don't understand, see if a glossary of terms has been provided for you. If there is a section that you don't understand, make a note of it; you might find the answer to your question a few pages later. When you are through reviewing the entire document, go over your list of questions. If you still don't understand an area or have some specific questions, call your software supplier and get the answer immediately.

Playaround Phase

After you have completed reviewing the documentation and have all of your questions answered, you are ready to put documentation and computer together.

You should enter some information and get an idea of what is required and how long each operation will take. You will, however, become faster at data entry the more you use the system. During this phase you should try everything! You have nothing to worry about, as there isn't anything you can damage. If there is, you should find out about it now. If there are month-end or year-end procedures, try them.

Keep the documentation handy. If you run across something that you don't understand, check the documentation. If need be, make notes or questions in the document. When you finish this phase, you should have a thorough understanding of the application.

If you find that you still have some questions, or if you find that there are areas that are still unclear, get in touch with your software supplier and get your questioned answered. If necessary, spend two or three sessions using this approach. Each time will give you a fuller understanding of the capabilities and limitations of the application.

Analyze Outputs

During your playaround phase you should be paying close attention to the various output reports available to you. Do they actually provide the information you need? Are they in a sequence that is going to be useful to you? Is the information correct? Is it complete? You may decide that you need additional information on a specific report. If you have used a third party, now is the time to contact them to determine if changes can be made, what they will cost, and how soon they can be done. You may have to modify your schedule based on your findings.

If you have contracted with a third party for your software, they will probably conduct a training session for you. You still should do as much on your own before that time as you can. These trainers can be thought of as instructors, but the real learning will come from your persistence and your efforts in applying what is taught.

CHAPTER 12

Mini-Test

The Importance of Testing Each Application

A mini-test is simply that —a small test of short duration used to double check the programs and the documentation to see if there is anything that either you or your third party forgot. The test time can range from only a few hours to a few weeks, depending on the complexity of the application you are testing. You will learn more about your computer with each application you test. You should plan to run a mini-test for each application you install. You will learn more about the application during these test phases than you will ever learn from simply reading the manual. And, you will learn it in the shortest period of time. You will also get a feel for the time required to accomplish data entry functions and the printing of appropriate reports.

I have had experience with accounts that refused to take the time for this step. They didn't feel they had the time available. Almost without exception, I would get a call a few weeks later and find out that the programs did not perform a crucial function that was necessary to their operation. Every business thinks that every other business does business the same way they do. They just can't understand why it wasn't part of the system. It always would happen when I was behind schedule and when they needed it most.

Setting Up Your Mini-Test

Setting up a mini-test is very simple. It merely requires that you, or one of your employees, select a small comprehensive set of information to test. If the application you wish to test is Payroll, you would select samples of employees covering all the different pay periods and rate types that you currently use, or intend to use, in the future. You may have salaried, hourly, commissioned, or a combination. They may be paid daily, weekly, biweekly, semimonthly, monthly, quarterly, etc.

After you have made your selection, simply enter the employee data, simulate a couple of your prior pay cycles, and compare the results.

If you are testing the Accounts Payable area, you would want to select some bills that would affect your expense items and some that would affect your inventory value. If you have an occasion to pay cash, receive discounts, or pre-pay bills, you would want to check them all out.

If you are getting ready to install the Accounts Receivable area, you would select some of your accounts receivable accounts that mirror a cross section of your receivables business. If your system offers different types, be sure to select one of each. In some receivable systems an inventory file is required. If this is true of your system, combine your inventory test with the receivable test.

The same principles apply to the Inventory area. If the system allows different inventory types, locations, status values, or categories, try them all. Choose items that were sold to the accounts that you selected for your accounts receivable test.

Once you have established your *base* for testing purposes, you are ready to begin entering the daily transactions. Your user's manual should tell you what to run on a daily, weekly, and monthly basis. Using your base data and entering your daily activity will allow you to get a feel for the application you are testing. Depending on the nature of the data entry functions, you may decide that it would be more efficient to redesign some of your own office forms. If it will save time or reduce the possibility of error, you should consider making the change before the final installation.

As you enter your daily transactions you can verify that the system is operating as documented and providing you with the information you need.

This is the time to find out about these things, not once you're trying to run live. You must also determine if the software meets with your expectations. Is there anything that you overlooked that is critical to the way you conduct your business? If you do find something, it is not too late to request that certain modifications be made before you begin running the system for real. If the programs can be modified to meet your needs, find out how long it will take. You may have to adjust your implementation schedule based on this information.

The more involved the application, the more time will be needed to run the mini-test. You should print every report that is available as part of the application. If there is a month-end process, you should run it, know why you are running it, and know what kind of results to expect. The same holds true for any daily or weekly processing.

Be sure to verify that any special forms required by the application area meet with your requirements. If you have them available, try them.

Once you have completed this mini-test you should know the application thoroughly. You are then ready to proceed to the next chapter.

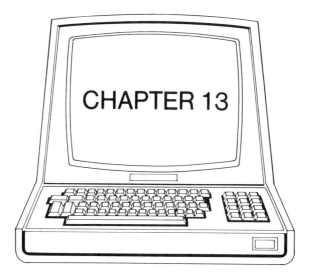

CHAPTER 13

Conversion

Getting Each Application Up—and Running

The time required for conversion of any application is, again, going to depend on the amount of data requiring conversion. The conversion of any application can be broken down into three basic steps: 1.) data collection, 2.) data entry, and 3.) data verification. It is difficult to determine the time involved in these operations without knowing the complexity of the system and the amount of data to be entered. If you are working with a third party, they can assist you in determining these times. The three areas mentioned above are discussed in the paragraphs that follow.

Data Collection

This function involves assembling the data for a specific application area and putting it in a format that will lend itself to rapid and easy input to the system.

I mentioned conversion forms earlier. *Conversion forms* are forms on which you simply write the information in the sequence that the computer will be asking for. If you are collecting the data for inventory and you have 1500 items, you may want to use some type of conversion form. If your software supplier did not supply them, you can probably make up your own. You, or you and your software supplier, can best determine if your data records are in a format that can be entered into the system easily and in a minimum amount of time.

In some cases, conversion forms might be a waste of time. If you have only ten employees and you are preparing to enter the employee data, making up a conversion form would be a waste of time, regardless of how the information is laid out for input. On the other hand, if you are getting ready for inventory (and the software system allows for a numeric item location) and if you have your items coded with a key for location, you have some homework to do.

The same is true of the Accounts Receivable area. You may feel that you don't need any conversion forms, but you do need to code your accounts as to type (commercial, public, institutional, etc.) or geographical location.

Data Entry

This function is the actual entry of the base data into the system. When I mention base data, I mean simply getting all the base information into the system. In the case of inventory, you would probably not want to enter the current quantities on hand because they would mostly change before you got everything loaded.

The base data is that data which is static in nature; that is, it doesn't change day to day. This would include product code, product types, description, location, etc.

Most systems allow for this initial generation of the base data. Then, when you are ready to go live, you take a quick inventory and enter the current balances. If the system you are using does not have this feature, you may want it added. Otherwise, you may have a long weekend ahead of you.

Data Verification

What this means is that after you have entered all your information, someone must verify the correctness of it. Again, based on the size of the data you are entering, this could take some time to accomplish. This is probably one of the most boring steps involved but one of the most important. There is a term common among programmers. It is four letters : GIGO, meaning "garbage in, garbage out." It is very important that the data you enter is 100 percent correct. If it is not, you cannot expect your systems to operate properly.

Final Installation

On Your Mark! Get Set!–GO!

You've finally reached the point where you've gotten to know your machine, you've run your mini-test, collected your data, and entered the base data. Now you're ready to go live! There's not much I can tell you at this point. If you've completed all the prior steps, this one should be a snap for you.

You will find this step is like many other steps in the application *installation* cycle. If your data is large, it will naturally take longer than if you are simply working with a few employee records.

If you are bringing up an inventory system of considerable size, you should probably schedule a Saturday to take your final inventory figures and enter them into the system. You then relax on Sunday, and you're ready to go on Monday.

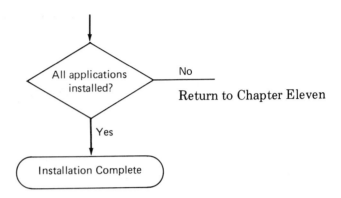

CHAPTER 15

Miscellaneous

My Nephew Ralph, Going It Alone, Back-ups, and General Ledger

In this chapter I have tried to discuss everything else that I've encountered in my experience that I thought would be helpful to you if you decide to automate your business. The book is really a step-by-step procedure to determine what you need and where to get it. The items in the following paragraphs just didn't fit into any of the other chapters. These are my feelings, so you can take them for what they're worth.

"My Nephew Can Write The Programs"

As I mentioned earlier, I've been in the computer field for over twenty years. I started out as a programmer and advanced in training and responsibility with a large software company for almost ten years. During that time, there were those that stayed as programmers! It's a fact that though some people are very good programmers, they are not capable of becoming analysts.

The analyst is the individual who can evaluate a set of user requirements and design a system. Anyone with the time and patience can learn the programming language and write a few simple programs, but writing 120 different programs that interact and feed information to other programs is not a simple task, especially for the novice. It takes many years of experience to acquire the necessary skills to create and program a complete system. If you're only looking for a few simple programs, you most likely don't need a computer.

Once again, if you have an employee or a nephew who knows programming, let him write some small one-time programs for you if you like. When it comes to something as important as your business, let the professional provide you with your software systems. In my experience I have run across a couple of clients who had tried to do it all on their own. In one case, the client purchased a machine from a local computer shop and then proceeded to buy some packages from a mail order company. When we finally ran across him, he had invested over $10,000 and an entire year of evenings and weekends. He eventually bought another computer from a major manufacturer and our software. He was up and running in a short period of time. One other individual wanted to buy our base system and modify it for a client of his. The result was also a disaster. The last report I got was that the company had hired a reliable third party to straighten out the mess.

My advice has always been that you're in the business you're in to make money. Trying to save money by doing it yourself is the worst way that I can think of. Undoubtedly you're good at what you do; otherwise, you wouldn't be in business. Being a computer programmer is a full-time job. If you want to be a programmer, then be one. Otherwise, leave it to the true professional.

General Ledger

Of all the areas that the businessman must deal with, this area is probably the least understood. I'm surprised at how many businessmen don't know how to read a profit-and-loss statement. Of all the applications that I installed (or assisted with), this area stands out as one of the biggest stumbling blocks.

It is not the responsibility of your software supplier to teach you, or any of your staff, the principles of accounting. In the first place, your third party is not an accountant and therefore cannot give you such advice! The individual you select for operating your computer must have some accounting background or knowledge if you plan to have an integrated system (one where the Payroll, Accounts Payable, Accounts Receivable, and Inventory areas feed the General Ledger system automatically). If the computer operator doesn't understand basic accounting, there is little chance that he will understand the system interaction of a fully integrated system. Buy yourself some basic accounting books or take a night course. It's important!

Off-Site Back-Ups

Almost without exception, every small business system will provide some means of backing up both your data and your programs. By backing up I mean the actual duplication of your information on a diskette or tape cartridge. You should plan to keep a copy of this information in at least one other location besides your office.

You should set up a standard procedure that every Friday (or Monday or whatever day you choose) you take a copy of your data files and your programs home with you. If you should be unfortunate and have a fire or some other catastrophe, you will have lost only a week's worth of information. You can take a back-up home with you every day if you wish. Then if some catastrophe should befall you, you simply have to get the use of another computer (like yours) and you will have not lost any of your valuable accounts receivable or other information.

CHAPTER 16

Conclusion

Some Final Thoughts!

If you've followed my advice and read the entire manual, you may think it sounds like a lot of work. You may even be considering scrapping the whole idea. If you have either concern I can only offer you a few words of advice—don't stop now!

You bought this book because you felt a need. You wanted to approach the task in a logical, systematic manner. This book provides that. By following the procedures described in this book I can guarantee that, if you proceed, you will be successful. The entire concept of this approach revolves around a few forms that you fill out. The written material in each chapter is really reference material to support the forms.

In years past the justification for a computer was based on how much money could be saved. A new approach, and quite valid, is utilizing a small business computer to make money.

The client who paid for both computer and software in three months is a prime example. His ability to charge interest to overdue accounts was profitable for him, and it can be for you, too. Time saved can also be considered as making money. With increased state and federal reporting requirements, some small businesses will not have a choice—they will have to computerize or get lost in the reporting requirements.

The client who runs five different companies on his small business computer reduced his bookkeeping and accounting functions from twelve hours a day to three hours a day.

Along with this drastic reduction he has, at his fingertips, information that allows him the control he never dreamed of. His total cost for the software (programs) was $7,500. He confided in me recently that knowing what he knows, he would have been willing to pay twice as much.

One tire dealer found the small business computer so efficient in terms of time savings, as well as money saved (earned), that he bought another computer exactly like the first. This client operates three stores in different towns. All billing and accounting functions are provided at the main store location on his twin computers. And he has not had to increase his office staff at all!

The fear that a computer will require the hiring of additional personnel is false. You can have all the benefits of a computer without having to hire additional trained personnel.

In most instances, a small business computer will actually free your office staff for other duties. Understand that this is not an immediate benefit. You must first go through the conversion and learning steps for each application.

The functions a computer can provide, for you and your business, are only limited by your imagination, time and money. Virtually anything is possible. Small business computers are full fledged computers, capable of accomplishing a wide range of applications.

The information contained in this book is the result of my twenty years of experience in the data processing field. *A Guide for Selecting Computers and Software for Small Businesses* was written for you, to assist you in the process of selecting both computer and software. If you follow the procedures outlined, apply them, and make that all-important personal commitment, then success will surely be yours.

Appendices

Appendix I

My Wish List

FOR: _____

WISH   AREA

_____   _____
_____   _____
_____   _____
_____   _____
_____   _____
_____   _____
_____   _____
_____   _____
_____   _____
_____   _____
_____   _____
_____   _____
_____   _____
_____   _____
_____   _____
_____   _____
_____   _____
_____   _____
_____   _____
_____   _____
_____   _____
_____   _____
_____   _____

Appendix II

Application Worksheet

FOR_____

APPLICATION AREAS*

1. _____
2. _____
3. _____
4. _____
5. _____
6. _____
7. _____
8. _____

*Listed in order of priority

SAMPLE APPLICATION AREAS

Accounts Receivable (A/R)
Invoicing (I)
Purchase Order Processing (POP)
Payroll (PAY)
Property Management (PM)
Mailing Label System (MLS)
Credit Union Accounting (CUA)
Client Writeup (CW)
Corporate Accounting (CA)

General Ledger (G/L)
Billing (B)
Inventory Control (IC)
Sales Analysis-A/R (SA/A)
Sales Analysis-IC (SA/I)
Job Costing (JC)
Distribution (D)
Partnership Accounting (PA)

Appendix III

Requirements Worksheet

FOR:_____

APPLICATION_____   PRIORITY:_____
REQUIREMENTS:

_____

_____

_____

_____

_____

_____

_____

_____

_____

_____

VOLUMES:

_____

_____

_____

_____

_____

Appendix IV

User Checklist (UC)

For:_____   DATE:_____

	N	Y	N/A
Have you determined the need?	___	___	___
Have you prioritized your application areas?	___	___	___
Have you completed the Requirements Worksheet?	___	___	___
Have you determined your business volumes?	___	___	___
Have you determined computer location?	___	___	___
Who will be responsible for your new computer?	___	___	___
If you choose an employee, have you talked to him/her?	___	___	___
Have you determined the best time to acquire your new computer?	___	___	___
Do you want a system that will handle multi-businesses?	___	___	___
Are you willing to change your way of doing certain things?	___	___	___
Have you made the commitment?	___	___	___

Appendix V

Hardware Salesman Checklist (HSC)

Name:_____   DATE:_____

	N	Y	N/A
Have you obtained at least three references?	___	___	___
Where is the location of the hardware maintenance?	___	___	___
Does the manufacturer provide on-site maintenance?	___	___	___
Computer maintenance cost, duration, and availability?	___	___	___
Is there a replacement machine available?	___	___	___
Will the computer handle your volumes?	___	___	___
Is there enough storage capacity for your data?	___	___	___
Is the storage capacity expandable?	___	___	___
Will there be hardware training at your office?	___	___	___
Are there training seminars?	___	___	___
Have you reviewed the training manuals?	___	___	___
Does the manufacturer provide software?	___	___	___
Does the computer require any special wiring?	___	___	___
Does the manufacturer provide utilities?	___	___	___
Is the computer upward compatible?	___	___	___
Is there a toll-free number to call for computer problems?	___	___	___
Is there an error book and can I understand it?	___	___	___

Appendix VI

Hardware Reference Questionnaire (HRQ)

Hardware Manufacturer: _____

Reference Name:_____ **Reference No.:**_____

Install Date:_____

	N	Y	N/A
How long has the computer been in operation?	___	___	___
What applications does the computer have?	___	___	___
Do you plan to add other applications?	___	___	___
How much of the day is the computer being used?	___	___	___
Has the computer proven reliable?	___	___	___
Has the computer ever been completely down?	___	___	___
How long did it take the maintenance man to respond?	___	___	___
How far away is the maintenance man?	___	___	___
Is there another machine close by?	___	___	___
Has the repair service been adequate?	___	___	___
Who operates the computer?	___	___	___
Is the computer easy to learn to use?	___	___	___
Who supplied the software?	___	___	___
Was the installation harder than expected?	___	___	___
Can you stop by to see the system in operation?	___	___	___
Have there been any electrical problems?	___	___	___
How would you rate the hardware documentation?	___	___	___
Have there been any problems with the computer location?	___	___	___
What did you find most difficult about the computer?	___	___	___

Appendix VII

Software Supplier Checklist (SSC)

Supplier Name:_____ **Date:**_____

	N	Y	N/A
Does their software meet your requirements?	___	___	___
Do you have a multi-business capability?	___	___	___
Do they provide simply a base package?	___	___	___
Are individual package pieces available?	___	___	___
Will they modify their package?	___	___	___
Have you determined the requirements of the modifications?	___	___	___
Is there a separate contract for modifications?	___	___	___
Have you determined a fixed cost for the modifications?	___	___	___
Have you determined a time frame for the modifications?	___	___	___
If they modify the programs will they update the documentation?	___	___	___
Can you review their documentation before signing a contract?	___	___	___
Is their documentation consistent?	___	___	___
Is their documentation clear?	___	___	___
Is there a guarantee that the system will do what the documentation says?	___	___	___
Will they modify any inconsistencies?	___	___	___
Is there a section devoted to error detection and recovery?	___	___	___
Are all output reports defined?	___	___	___
Is on-site training provided?	___	___	___
How much on-site training will you get?	___	___	___

Appendix VII (cont.)

Is additional training available? ___ ___ ___

What will additional training cost? ___ ___ ___

Is after-hours training available? ___ ___ ___

Are system enhancements and updates free? ___ ___ ___

Who installs these free enhancements? ___ ___ ___

Is the third party local or do they have a local
representative? ___ ___ ___

Is phone consultation available? ___ ___ ___

What type of telephone service and/or response
can I expect? ___ ___ ___

Do they have back-up support? ___ ___ ___

Do they have a "starter-pac" of forms? ___ ___ ___

Are there a variety of special forms from which
to choose? ___ ___ ___

Do they provide conversion forms? ___ ___ ___

Do they provide conversion assistance? ___ ___ ___

What kind of maintenance contracts do they
provide? ___ ___ ___

Does their system provide for automatic back-up
procedures? ___ ___ ___

Do they provide or will they assist you in
establishing an implementation plan? ___ ___ ___

Have they provided you with all contracts? ___ ___ ___

Have you obtained the three references? ___ ___ ___

Appendix VIII

Software Reference Questionnaire (SRQ)

Software Provider:_____

Reference Name:_____Reference Phone:_____

Applications_____

	N	Y	N/A
What applications did you originally plan to install?	___	___	___
Did you get installed what you had originally planned?	___	___	___
Did you find the system easy to learn?	___	___	___
Is the documentation consistent with the programs?	___	___	___
How long did it take you to get up and running?	___	___	___
Did it take you longer than you were led to believe?	___	___	___
Did the programs live up to the sales pitch?	___	___	___
What has been the response to any problems that you encountered?	___	___	___
Are they knowledgeable in general business practices?	___	___	___
Did they help you with the conversion?	___	___	___
Did they work well with your employees?	___	___	___
Were there any hidden costs?	___	___	
Have they completed the job to your satisfaction?	___	___	___
If you had it to do all over again, would you?	___	___	___
Would it be possible to stop by and see your system?	___	___	___

Appendix IX

Scheduling Worksheet

FOR:_____

MONTH
DAY

FUNCTIONS
  Computer Arrives
  Machine Familiarization

  APPLICATION (   )
    Training
    Test Data Selection
    Mini-Test
    Review Test
    Data Collection
    Conversion
    Installation

  APPLICATION (   )
    Training
    Test Data Selection
    Mini-Test
    Review Test
    Data Collection
    Conversion
    Installation

Glossary of Terms Used in This Book

Access—The ability to use a computer.

Address—The location in computer memory where a given binary bit of information is stored.

Alphanumeric—The set of punctuation, letters of the alphabet, and numeric characters often used for computer input.

Application—A series of interrelated activities. As used in this book, Payroll, Accounts Receivable, etc. are application areas.

ASCII—The American Standard Code for Information Exchange.

Assembly Language—A low-level symbolic programming language which comes closest to programming a computer in its internal machine language.

Audio Cassette Interface (ACR)—A circuit which allows computer data to be audibly stored on a standard cassette tape with a standard recorder.

Automation—The generalized term used to convey the dedicated use of automatic machines (computer) to control various processes, routine office procedures, accounting, and thousands of other applications.

Base Package—A set of computer programs used as a starting point from which modifications will be made to fulfill a user's requirements.

Binary—The number system of base two which has two symbols: 0 and 1, representing the off and on status of a circuit.

Bit—A single binary digit.

Byte—A group of bits (usually eight for microcomputers). The memory capacity of a computer is usually measured in terms of bytes.

Canned Demonstration—A set of programs, procedures, data, and activities designed specifically for a predefined reason.

Chip—An integrated circuit.

Compiler—A program which converts the program statements of a high-level language into machine codes for execution.

Computer—The equipment which accepts programs to execute the instructions of the program.

Computer program—A set of instructions written in a language designed for ease of use in communicating with a computer.

Computer Store—Any business dealing with the selling of a specific brand of computer or different brands over the counter.

Computer System—See Software System.

Conversion—The process of changing information from one form of representation (ex., file cards) to be processed by a computer (ex., diskettes, magnetic tape, etc.).

Conversion Forms—Forms designed to sequence information in an order which will allow rapid entry into a computer.

CPU (Central Processing Unit)—The major operations center of a computer where decisions and calculations are made.

Data—Computer-coded information.

Data Entry—The process of entering information into a computer.

Data Processing Professional—An individual schooled in areas relating to computers and programs.

Debug—The removal of program errors (bugs) from a computer program.

Digital—A circuit which has only two states: on and off, and is usually represented by the binary number system.

Diskettes—Small, record-like objects, magnetized to store information. They are inexpensive, take up little space, and can store a vast amount of information. (Also referred to as "floppies.")

Documentation—Related to all the manuals and written material associated with computers and computer programs.

DOS (Disc Operating System)—Allows the use of general commands to manipulate data stored on a disk.

Equipment—As used in this book, any combination of computers, printers, display tubes, etc.

First Party—You, the user.

Flow Diagram—A chart to represent, for a specific problem, the flow of data, methods, steps, procedures, etc.

Functional Area—An area defined to accomplish specific procedures, routines, etc.

Hardware—Any combination of computers, printers, display terminals, and other related equipment.

Hardware Manufacturers—The companies who build computers and related equipment.

Hardware Vendor—The individual or company that provides the computer and related equipment.

Hexadecimal—A base sixteen number system often used in programming in machine language.

Input—Information (data) fed into the computer.

Input/Output (I/O) Devices—Peripheral hardware devices which communicate to or receive communications from the computer.

Installation—The process of setting up computers or programs in a user location.

Interface—A device which converts electronic signals such that two devices may communicate with each other.

Interpreter—A program which accepts one statement at one time of a high-level language, converts that statement to machine language, and proceeds to the next statement.

Languages—The set of words/commands which are understood by the computer. (Used in writing a program.)

Machine—As used in this book, any combination of computers, printers, display tubes, and information storage devices.

Machine Language—The internal language of the computer.

Mainframe—Referring to the hardware of the central processing unit (CPU).

Memory—Data (information) stored for future reference by the computer in a series of bytes.

Microcomputer—A miniaturized small computer containing all the circuitry of a minicomputer on a single integrated circuit chip.

Microprocessor—The single integrated circuit chip which forms the basis of a microcomputer (the CPU).

Modem—A peripheral device which converts digital signals to audio and vice-versa.

Opcode—An operation code signifying a particular task to be done by the computer.

Package—A set of computer programs which may include a number of applications which have been combined into a package.

Parallel Test—The act of running two tests simultaneously and comparing the results. (Ex., running a computer test to verify some results as normal office procedures.)

Peripherals—Input/Output devices such as printers, mass storage devices, terminals, etc.

Printer—An output device for spelling out computer results as words, numbers, or symbols.

Program—A set of instructions written in a language designed for ease of use in communicating with a computer and solving a wide variety of problems.

Programmer—One who prepares programs for a computer.

Programming—The art of reducing the plan for the solution of a problem to machine-sensible instructions.

RAM (Random Access Memory)—Memory devices from which data may be procured or stored by the computer.

ROM (Read Only Memory)—Memory devices from which data may be procured only; the memory contents may not be changed.

Second Party—Normally the computer salesman.

Service Bureau—A data processing organization which offers a wide range of computer services to businesses or organizations.

Small Business Computer—Low-cost computers designed for ease in learning and operations.

Software—The internal programs or routines professionally prepared to simplify various computer operations.

Software, Salesman—See Software Vendor.

Software, Supplier—See Software Vendor.

Software System—A collection of computer programs united to accomplish a specific objective.

Software Vendor—Individuals or companies that distribute software systems (i.e., computer programs).

Special Forms—Any form used by the system other than the standard size. Could include: statements, invoices, payroll checks, etc.

Specialty Software—Programs or routines written with specific industry in mind.

Statement—A single computer instruction.

Storage Capacity—The amount of information that can be retained in the memory of a computer.

Subroutine—A smaller program (routine) within a larger program.

Symbol, Flow Chart—Symbols used to represent operations, data, and equipment in data processing problems.

System—A collection of operations (applications) united to accomplish a specific objective.

System, Back-up—Refers to the process of duplicating processing programs and data files in the event of primary equipment failure.

System Enhancement—The modification of programs to accomplish an improvement in any function.

System Requirement—The actual or anticipated questions that may be requested of a software system.

Terminal—An Input/Output device using a keyboard and video or printer display.

Third Party—Normally refers to the party who provides the computer programs.

Upward Compatible—The ability to move up to a larger computer without extensive changes to the computer programs.

User—The person or company using a computer or the services of data processing professionals.

Utilities—A term used to define a wide range of functions such as: data conversion, editing, file manipulation, computer diagnostic routines, etc.

Word—A basic unit of computer memory usually expressed in terms of a byte.

Selected Bibliographies

Berger, Melvin. "Those Amazing Computers." New York: The John Day Company, 1973. A brief history of computers, how they work, and the relationship between the human brain and the electronic brain.

Rusch, Richard B. "Computers: Their History and How They Work." Simon & Schuster, Inc., 1969. A history of computers and how they work. Covers machine languages, central processing units, storage media, and data communication devices.

Sipple, Charles. and Dahl, Fred. "Computer Power For the Small Business." Englewood Cliffs, N.J.: Prentice Hall, Inc., 1979. A broad, generalized book at computer systems for the small business.

Sipple, Charles J. and Sippl, Charles P. "Computer Dictionary and Handbook." Indianapolis: Howard W. Sams & Co., 1972. Complete dictionary of computer terms plus an indepth discussion of computer systems, languages, mathematical definitions, etc.

Index